P9-BBM-704

JAMIE OLIVER'S MEALS IN MINUTES

Also by Jamie Oliver

The Naked Chef

The Return of the Naked Chef

Happy Days with the Naked Chef

Jamie's Kitchen

Jamie's Dinners

Jamie's Italy

Cook with Jamie

Jamie at Home

Jamie's Ministry of Food

Jamie's America

JAMIE OLIVER'S MEALS IN MINUTES

Photography by
DAVID LOFTUS

HYPERION
NEW YORK

Published by arrangement with Michael Joseph / The Penguin Group

www.penguin.com
www.jamieoliver.com

Copyright © Jamie Oliver, 2010, 2011
Photography copyright © David Loftus, 2010, 2011

All rights reserved. No part of this book may be used or reproduced in any manner
whatsoever without the written permission of the Publisher. Printed in Italy.
For information address Hyperion, 114 Fifth Avenue, New York,
New York 10011.

ISBN: 978-1-4013-2442-1

Hyperion books are available for special promotions and premiums.
For details contact the HarperCollins Special Markets Department
in the New York office at 212-207-7528, fax 212-207-7222,
or email spsales@harpercollins.com.

First U.S. Edition

10 9 8 7 6 5 4 3 2 1

jamieoliver.com

SIMON LAURENCE KINDER
7 April 1962 – 16 May 2010

I dedicate this book to Simon Kinder, a dear friend of mine who has sadly passed away. He was the Managing Director of Magimix UK and one of the very best and most loved figures in the food industry. He was certainly one of my favorite people to be around, and his passion for food and friendship was always appreciated. He'll be sorely missed by me and my team, as well as all of his staff at Magimix. Our love goes out to his wonderful children, Max and Katya, their mother, Monica, and to all of his family.

He would have loved this book because we use food processors and liquidizers left, right and center to make it speedy. Bless him.

THE MEALS

BROCCOLI ORECCHIETTE   zucchini & bocconcini salad, prosciutto & melon salad   24

PREGNANT JOOLS'S PASTA   crunchy red endive & watercress salad, little frangipane tarts   30

CAULIFLOWER MACARONI   Belgian endive salad with insane dressing, lovely stewed fruit   34

TRAPANI-STYLE RIGATONI   griddled Belgian endive salad, arugula & Parmesan salad, limoncello kinda trifle   40

WONKY SUMMER PASTA   herby salad, pear drop tartlets   44

SUMMER VEGGIES LASAGNE   Tuscan tomato salad, quick mango frozen yogurt in baby cones   48

SPAGHETTI ALLA PUTTANESCA   crunchy salad, garlic bread, silky chocolate ganache   54

CHEAT'S PIZZA   3 delish salads, squashed cherries & vanilla mascarpone cream   58

OOZY MUSHROOM RISOTTO   spinach salad, quick lemon & raspberry cheesecake   64

SPINACH & FETA FILO PIE   cucumber salad, tomato salad, coated ice cream   70

TOMATO SOUP   chunky croutons, crunchy veggies and guacamole, sticky prune sponge desserts   76

CURRY ROGAN JOSH   fluffy rice, carrot salad, pappadams, flatbread   80

GREEN CURRY   crispy chicken, kimchee slaw, rice noodles   86

CHICKEN PIE   French-style peas, sweet carrot smash, berries, shortbread & Chantilly cream   90

MUSTARD CHICKEN   quick dauphinoise, greens, Black Forest affogato   96

TRAY-BAKED CHICKEN   squashed potatoes, creamed spinach, strawberry slushie   102

KILLER JERK CHICKEN   rice & beans, refreshing chopped salad, chargrilled corn   106

CHICKEN SKEWERS   amazing Satay sauce, fiery noodle salad, fruit & mint sugar   110

STUFFED CYPRIOT CHICKEN   pan-fried asparagus & vine tomatoes, cabbage salad, St. Clement's drink, vanilla ice cream float   116

PIRI PIRI CHICKEN   dressed potatoes, arugula salad, quick Portuguese tarts   120

DUCK SALAD   giant croutons, cheat's rice pudding with stewed fruit   126

THAI RED SHRIMP CURRY   jasmine rice, cucumber salad, papaya platter   130

GRILLED SARDINES   crispy halloumi, watercress salad & figs, thick chocolate mousse   134

TASTY CRUSTED COD   my mashy peas, tartar sauce, warm garden salad   140

SWEDISH-STYLE FISHCAKES   roasted baby potatoes, sprout salad, fresh zingy salsa   146

STICKY PAN-FRIED SCALLOPS   sweet chili rice, dressed greens, quick brownies   150

SERIOUSLY GOOD FISH TAGINE   fennel & lemon salad, couscous, orange & mint tea   154

SMOKED SALMON   potato salad, beets & cottage cheese, rye bread & homemade butter   160

FINNAN HADDIE CORN CHOWDER   spiced shrimp, rainbow salad, raspberry & elderflower slushie   164

FISH TRAY-BAKE   baby potatoes, salsa verde, simple spinach salad, cheat's banoffee pie   168

BLOODY MARY MUSSELS   herby salad, gorgeous rhubarb millefeuille   174

BRANZINO & CRISPY PANCETTA   mashed sweet potatoes, Asian greens, 1-minute berry ice cream, sparkling lemon ginger drink   180

ASIAN-STYLE SALMON   noodle broth, bean sprout salad, lychee dessert   186

CRISPY SALMON   jazzed-up rice, baby zucchini salad, gorgeous guacamole, berry spritzer   190

ROAST BEEF   baby popovers, little carrots, crispy potatoes, super-quick gravy   194

STEAK SARNIE   crispy baby potatoes, cheesy mushrooms, beet salad   200

RIB-EYE STIR-FRY   dan dan noodles, chilled hibiscus tea   204

SUPER-FAST BEEF HASH   baked potatoes, goddess salad, lovely butter beans & bacon   210

STEAK INDIAN-STYLE   spinach & paneer salad, naan breads, mango dessert   216

MEATBALL SANDWICH   pickled cabbage, chopped salad, banana ice cream   220

LIVER & BACON   onion gravy, smashed potatoes, dressed greens, berry & custard ripple   226

STUFFED FOCACCIA   prosciutto, celery root remoulade, dressed mozzarella, fresh lemon & lime granita   230

SEARED PORK FILLET & CATHERINE WHEEL SAUSAGE   meaty mushroom sauce, celery root smash, garlicky beans   236

PORK CHOPS & CRISPY CRACKLINS   crushed potatoes, minty cabbage, peaches 'n' custard   240

KINDA SAUSAGE CASSOULET   warm broccoli salad, meringues   244

BRITISH PICNIC   sausage rolls, mackerel pâté, lovely asparagus, crunch salad, Pimm's Eton mess   250

CATHERINE WHEEL SAUSAGE   horseradish mashed potatoes, apple salad, sage & leek gravy, stuffed apples   256

TAPAS FEAST   tortilla, glazed chorizo, manchego cheese, cured meats & honey, stuffed sweet peppers, rolled anchovies   260

MOROCCAN LAMB CHOPS   flatbreads, herby couscous, stuffed sweet peppers, pomegranate drink   264

SPRING LAMB   vegetable platter, mint sauce, Chianti gravy, chocolate fondue   268

I'M TOO BUSY . . . IT'S TOO EXPENSIVE . . . I DON'T KNOW HOW . . .

These are the three excuses I always hear when I ask people why they don't cook at home more often. But I know that with the right equipment, some organization, and solid recipes, these excuses don't stand up. Regardless of whether you're a brilliant cook or a complete beginner, this book does what it says on the can. I honestly believe that if you embrace these meals, they will change the way you cook, forever.

The most revolutionary thing about the meals in this book is not that they can be cooked quickly (they can), and it's not that they use loads of clever shortcuts and tricks (they do), it's that I've written them in a completely unique way. I'm going to walk you through every step needed to create a whole meal, so in 20 to 30 minutes you will be putting beautiful main dishes, exciting sides and salads, lovely drinks and desserts on the table at the same time—all from one recipe! I've come up with 50 incredible meals for you: meaty ones, vegetarian meals, quick pastas and desserts, lovely curries and things you might never have thought achievable in this short amount of time.

I want this book to help skyrocket you to another level, where you can nourish yourself and your family, and cook quickly, with a real sense of style. I'm going to ask you to use your kitchen in a completely new way, but it's different, it's fun, and the results will blow you away.

YOU DO HAVE THE TIME

You may be the busiest person in the world, but you still need to eat. In just 20 to 30 minutes – about the same amount of time it takes to warm up a heat-and-serve meal in the oven, watch something on TV, or order and pick up a take-out meal—I want to show you that you can have an amazing home-cooked spread on the table.

I recently realized that the way I was cooking during the week wasn't very efficient. Because I can cook, I often freestyle my meals and make things up as I go, but this has meant that although the food tasted great, my approach was slightly chaotic and I ended up spending more time in the kitchen, and more time washing up, when I could have been putting the kids to bed and reading them a story. So I started making a plan and approaching Monday to Thursday's meals methodically. I haven't looked back.

Of course on weekends I slow the pace down and really take my time in the kitchen, but with the week being such a busy time, it helps to be organized when it comes to shopping and cooking so you can have more fun with your free time. Family time seems to come way down the priority list these days, so I hope that learning how to get beautiful, quick meals on the table will help to bring more people back together at mealtimes.

IT'S NOT TOO EXPENSIVE

I didn't set out to make this a budget cookbook; there are meals in here to satisfy the foodiest of foodies! But, because I was curious, I costed these meals against their store-bought equivalents on main street, and it turns out that most of them are actually cheaper to make from scratch than they are to buy from your local take-out restaurant or frozen-entrée supermarket aisle. Just think: you can sit down with your favorite people in your own home and enjoy a fantastic spread for less than you'd spend anywhere else; you'll know exactly what went into it and it will be better for you. Just brilliant!

I've also discovered loads of cool tips and tricks by cooking this way which I've included in the recipes—I hope that they will help you to become a faster, more intelligent cook, no matter what you're making. In the long run, this will also help to save you money because you'll be able to cook anything from scratch in no time at all.

I'M GOING TO SHOW YOU HOW

These recipes are carefully choreographed so that no single minute is wasted. I've taken care of all the awkward, difficult stuff like menu planning and timing for you; all you have to do is follow my instructions, move quickly, and enjoy the ride. If at first you run a little over time and your kitchen is a bit messy, please don't worry—it's all part of the process, and you will radically improve the more you make these meals. Remember, this is about cooking in a whole new way. Like riding a bike, learning to drive, or making "beautiful love," you might not always get things right first time around, but the benefits when you finally crack it are incredible!

There's no denying that this is an energetic workhorse of a book. These 50 meals are going to keep you busy and make you multi-task, but you'll soon get used to it, and even find it slightly addictive. I don't want you to freestyle your way through the recipes, swap in different elements (at least not at the beginning), or use ingredients and measurements other than the ones I've used here, because they've been tested by my food team, my gang in the office, and even complete strangers, so I know they work. Of course there will be nights when you just want to curl up on the sofa with your missus or mister and have a simple bowl of pasta or salad, and if that's the case you can pick and choose your favorite elements from these meals, as they are clearly laid out and easy to extract. But this book is all about cooking meals, so on those weeknights or busy weekends when everyone is together, remember that with less than half an hour of organized energy, you can create something truly special.

In order to knock these meals out quickly, I want you to get into the Meals in Minutes frame of mind, which is all about organizing your kitchen and your equipment. On the next few pages I've outlined everything you need to do to make this happen. This is important stuff and it's there to help you, so please read it all before starting any of the recipes. See it as a call to action, and get excited about it!

You'll find that I'm being direct and to the point throughout the book, but there's good reason for that. I want you to end up with two things we all crave: beautiful, tasty food that shocks you because it's so good, and more time to spend with the people you love. So go on, and have fun with it!

Jamie O xx

PS When you see this symbol in the recipes go to www.jamieoliver.com/Meals, where you'll find a helpful video of that technique in the how-to section. There are also loads more great videos on my website (including one on knife skills), step-by-step pictures, hints, tips, and all sorts of wonderful bonus material to help you become a lean, mean cooking machine.

RECLAIM YOUR KITCHEN FOR THE JOB IT WAS MEANT FOR!

Too many of us are trying to cook dinner with children's toys under our feet, magazines on the table, bills stacked up on our kitchen worktops, and bags, keys, laundry, shoes, and other bits of clutter around us. But that's all about to change, because my goal is to help you make your kitchen as pared-back, lean, and relevant to its job as possible so that you can smash out incredible food any night of the week. Don't let the other rooms in your house invade your cooking space: if you see any of the clutter I'm talking about in your kitchen, find another home for it.

Sort out your equipment

Put aside an hour or two and pull out all of your kitchen equipment. How much of it do you use? What bits of equipment from the essential list on page 21 do you need? If you come across massive pans or fancy kitchen gadgets you only use once or twice a year, put them into storage or well out of the way. Once this is done, your cooking will flow so much better.

Arrange it sensibly

Before you cook one of these meals, read through the recipe to identify the other smaller bits of equipment you're going to need. Set everything out so it's on hand when you need it, and think through the recipe. If you know you're going to need to put something into the freezer, make sure you've got the space before you start, so you don't get tripped up.

I find it really helpful to keep larger utensils, like tongs, spatulas, and wooden spoons, in a big jar next to the stove so they're easy to reach when I'm cooking, but do whatever works best for you in the space you've got. Clear mason jars are fantastic for pantry ingredients like flour, sugar, spices, and herbs, because you can find the stuff you need right away.

Clear as you go

Cooking these meals is going to be busy and fast-paced, so having a trash can or a large bowl for garbage next to you as you prep is a great idea. Working into a clear sink or dishwasher as you go is also going to help keep your kitchen from looking like a bomb site after the meal is finished. These tips might sound basic, but they will make all the difference.

Make room for the meal

Clear your table before you start cooking. If it's cluttered, your lovely hot food is going to sit waiting while you sort it out. So clear it before you start and you'll be ready to cook some serious meals.

A QUICK WORD ABOUT INGREDIENTS

Over your lifetime, you'll spend more money on food than almost anything else. It's important to be "foodwise" because the reality is that not everyone out there is selling great food.

I believe it's important to eat eggs, chicken, and meat from farms that treat animals in an ethical way. This means not cramming egg-laying hens into horrible "battery cages" and giving chickens and animals time and space to grow properly. Animals reared in an ethical way might cost a little more, but I'd rather eat better meat less often than eat cheap, mass-produced meat every day. Believe me, it tastes miles better.

How you spend your dollars is massively political. If you start to ask questions and spend your money *slightly* differently, the huge industries that want your dollar will diversify and improve their welfare standards. The way you think about food will create the world in the future, so it's right that you should question where the ingredients are coming from.

Eggs, chicken, and meat: Look for labeling that tells you these products have come from ethical or "higher welfare" sources. This means eggs from hens that have been able to move around, have had access to natural light, and have been able to display natural behavior. Unfortunately, most eggs come from battery-caged hens, so look for terms like "cage free," "cruelty free," "free range," or "organic." The same goes for meat, especially pork. You want meat from animals that have lived in conditions with space, natural light, and good feed. It's also worth mentioning that products containing eggs, like mayonnaise, store-bought meringues, pre-made pastry cases, or even egg noodles, sometimes use free-range eggs too, so definitely look for those.

Fish: "Sustainability" refers to the long-term impact of taking fish from the sea. It's complicated because something that is overfished in one part of the world might be thriving elsewhere, but make an effort to find out what the situation is in your area. If a certain type of fish is under threat, shop for a more plentiful variety.

For more good information on these issues, check out websites like www.animalwelfare approved.org, or look at www.jamieoliver.com/mealsinminutes.

YOU NEED THIS EQUIPMENT

Because it's my duty to help you achieve the meals in this book quickly and efficiently, I'm going to be straight with you: you've GOT to have the gear listed opposite in order to make the meals in this book in around 20 to 30 minutes. Without certain bits of equipment, like a food processor, blender, or electric kettle, you simply won't be able to work fast enough.

I've priced the whole lot on various home-supply websites and (as of the month this book went to print) if you're starting from scratch you can get absolutely everything on the list for around $550. That includes a food processor and a microwave, each for around $60, and a blender for $20 (about the same price as a small round of pints at the pub). Of course the products on those sites range from very cheap and basic to top-of-the-line gear, and everything in between. Whether you want to spend the bare minimum or invest a lot more, accumulating all this equipment should not be seen as an unachievable goal. Start off with what you can and build the rest up over time, because the more you have, the more of these meals you'll be able to make and the faster and better your cooking will get.

Personally, when it comes to things like knives, pans, and electrical equipment I think it's well worth spending a bit more and getting something decent that will last. So save up, or use birthdays, holidays, or your wedding list to blag the bits you're missing. If you don't have a garlic press or a vegetable peeler, skip your morning cappuccino or two and use that money to buy one.

Most of us eat three times a day, every day of our lives. Spending money on prepackaged food, take-out, or fast food because you don't want to invest the money in your own kitchen is a false economy. I know this equipment will pay for itself 100 times over in the long run, so please—for the sake of yourself, your family, and your future dinner guests—prioritize your kitchen. If you don't, you're only cheating yourself.

A QUICK WORD ABOUT MICROWAVES

Microwaves have sort of become synonymous with pre-prepared meals, so including one on my equipment list is definitely a first for me! But I've read that over 90 percent of homes in the U.S. have a microwave, so it would be mad for me to think you don't have one. In this book, you're going to be using your microwave to free up space on the stove and help you cook fresh, tasty food. The recipes in this book have all been tested using an 800W microwave, so you may need to adjust your timings or power levels depending on the wattage of yours.

THE LIST

Food processor with the following attachments: standard blade, thick and thin slicer discs, fine and coarse graters, whisk, and beater

Blender

Microwave

Hand blender with a whisk attachment

Electric kettle

Large grill pan (approx. 10 x 12 inches)

Large non-stick ovenproof frying pan with lid (approx. 12 inches)

Medium non-stick frying pan with lid (approx. 10 inches)

Small non-stick frying pan with lid (approx. 8 inches)

Large deep saucepan with lid (approx. 10 inches)

Medium saucepan with lid (approx. 8 inches)

Small saucepan with lid (approx. 7 inches)

3-level steamer pan

Large deep sturdy half sheet pan (approx. 13 x 18 inches)

Medium roasting pan with wire rack

Baking pan (approx. 9 x 13 inches)

Non-stick baking sheet

6-cup muffin pan

12-cup muffin pan

3 good-quality knives: chef's knife, paring knife, bread knife

2 plastic cutting boards

2 large wooden cutting boards

Nest of mixing bowls

Colander

Fine strainer

Pestle and mortar

Garlic press

Tongs

Slotted spatula

Wooden spoons

Ladle

Slotted spoon

Spatula

Potato masher

Y-peeler (or, as I like to call it, "speed-peeler")

Box grater

Fine handheld grater

Measuring jug

Cup measures

Measuring spoons

Balloon whisk

Can opener

Rolling pin

Pastry brush

Bottle opener

Ice cream scoop

Aluminum foil, parchment paper

Microwave-safe plastic wrap

FAMILY-STYLE SHARING

This book is full of food you're going to share with your family and friends, and for that reason I see the table as the heart and soul of my *Meals in Minutes*. All the lovely dishes you create are going to come together here in one beautiful spread, and eating them together should be a fun, sociable experience. Because my job is to make you look good, I've given you a list below of some of the bits and pieces I use for serving all the time. These things aren't essential in the same way as the kitchen gear, but to my mind they are incredibly important because they are going to help you create an exciting-looking table people want to sit around.

- Platters of all shapes and sizes—new or antique, whichever style you wish

- Beautiful large serving bowls that work for salads, soups, vegetables, and desserts

- Large wooden cutting boards that look good enough to double as serving boards

- Mats, boards, or even cute ceramic tiles to put trays and pans on so you can take them directly from the oven to the table

- Frying pans and saucepans that look good enough to go straight to the table (it's worth bearing this in mind when you shop for pans, so they can do two jobs for you)

- Teacups or cappuccino cups that can double as little dessert bowls (I think it's quite sweet when they're mismatched)

- Large beer glasses or jars to put flatware in (who says you have to set the table every night?)

- Little bowls for sauces and dips

- Gravy boats and little glass pitchers for gravies and dressings

- A nice big 1-quart pitcher for drinks

BROCCOLI ORECCHIETTE

ZUCCHINI &

BOCCONCINI SALAD

PROSCIUTTO &

MELON SALAD

SERVES 6

PASTA
5 ounces Parmesan cheese
1 large head of broccoli
7 ounces broccolini
1 x 2-ounce can anchovies in oil
1 heaped tablespoon capers, drained
1 small dried chile
3 cloves garlic
a few sprigs of fresh thyme
1 pound dried orecchiette

ZUCCHINI SALAD
3 large sprigs of fresh mint
½ fresh red chile
1 lemon
8 ounces baby zucchini, mixed colors
4 ounces bocconcini di mozzarella (baby mozzarella balls)

SEASONINGS
olive oil
extra virgin olive oil
sea salt & black pepper

PROSCIUTTO & MELON SALAD
a small bunch of fresh basil
½ lemon
8 ounces prosciutto
1 cantaloupe
balsamic vinegar

TO START Get all your ingredients and equipment ready. Put the fine grater attachment into the food processor. Fill and boil the kettle. Put a large frying pan on a low heat.

PASTA Trim the rind off your Parmesan and set aside. Grate the chunk of Parmesan in the food processor, then tip into a bowl. Slice all the florets off the stalk of the large head of broccoli. Trim off the florets from the broccolini and chop up just the tender stalks. Put all the broccoli to one side.

Fit the standard blade attachment to the processor. Halve the large broccoli stalk and put into the empty processor with the anchovies and their oil, and the drained capers. Crumble in the dried chile. Peel and add the 3 cloves garlic, then pulse it all to a paste. Pour the boiled water into a large deep saucepan and put on a high heat.

Put about 3 tablespoons of olive oil into the large frying pan and spoon in the broccoli paste. Stir, then pick and tear in some thyme leaves, discarding the woody stalks. Pour a wineglass of water into the pan and add the reserved Parmesan rind. Give it a good stir and turn the heat up to medium. Keep your eye on it, stirring every now and then. Half-fill the kettle and reboil.

Add the orecchiette to the saucepan of boiling water with a pinch of salt and cook following the package instructions, with the lid askew. Now you've got about 12 minutes of pasta cooking time to make your 2 salads, so crack on!

ZUCCHINI SALAD Pick the mint leaves over a cutting board. Add ½ a red chile. Zest over ½ the lemon, then chop the chile and mint together until really fine. Spoon into the middle of a serving platter, drizzle over about 3 tablespoons of extra virgin olive oil, and squeeze in the juice of ½ the lemon. Add a pinch of salt & pepper, then taste and adjust the flavors if necessary. Peel the zucchini into ribbons over this dressing. Drain the container of baby mozzarella, then tip over the zucchini and take to the table to toss and dress at the last minute.

PASTA Give the pasta a stir and top up with more water from the kettle, if needed. After 5 minutes add all the reserved broccoli florets and the chopped broccolini stalks to the pasta with a splash of water from the kettle.

PROSCIUTTO & MELON SALAD Pick the leaves from the basil, setting the smaller ones aside for later. Put the big leaves into a pestle & mortar with a pinch of salt and bash to a paste. Add 2 tablespoons of extra virgin olive oil, plus a good squeeze of lemon juice. Lay 12 slices of prosciutto on a platter, leaving a space in the middle. Halve the melon, spoon out the seeds, then use a spoon to quickly scoop chunks of flesh into the middle of the platter. Drizzle over a little balsamic, then scatter over the reserved small basil leaves. Squeeze the juices from the melon halves into the dressing and stir in, then take the platter to the table, with the mortar and a spoon for drizzling over the dressing.

PASTA Drain the pasta and broccoli in a colander, reserving some of the cooking water, and add to the frying pan of paste. Fish out the Parmesan rind and discard. Add a big handful or two of grated Parmesan and a ladle or two of the cooking water. Carefully and quickly stir around and keep it moving until you achieve shiny, loose, lovely pasta. Taste and correct the seasoning, then tip onto a serving platter and sprinkle over a handful of Parmesan. Drizzle with extra virgin olive oil and scatter over the rest of the small reserved basil leaves. Take to the table with the rest of the Parmesan for sprinkling over.

TO SERVE When everyone is ready to eat, use 2 forks to toss the zucchini ribbons and baby mozzarella. Serve next to some of that lovely pasta and the prosciutto and melon salad.

PREGNANT JOOLS'S PASTA

CRUNCHY RED ENDIVE & WATERCRESS SALAD

LITTLE FRANGIPANE TARTS

SERVES 6

PASTA

4 scallions
1 carrot
1 stalk celery
1–2 fresh red chiles
6 good-quality sausages
  (approx. 14 ounces)
1 heaping teaspoon fennel seeds
1 teaspoon dried oregano
1 pound dried penne
4 cloves garlic
¼ cup balsamic vinegar
1 x 14-ounce can diced tomatoes
a few sprigs of Greek basil, or
  regular basil

SALAD

2 heads red endive, or 1 large
  head radicchio
4 cups (8 ounces) prewashed
  arugula and watercress
Parmesan cheese, for shaving over
1 lemon

SEASONINGS

olive oil
extra virgin olive oil
sea salt & black pepper

TARTS

6 individual-size ready-to-use pie
  shells*
1 egg
1 cup almond meal (flour)
7 tablespoons butter
½ cup superfine sugar
1 orange
1 tablespoon vanilla paste or extract
¾ cup good-quality raspberry
  preserve
1 cup crème fraîche, to serve

*If you can't find small pastry shells,
use a 9-inch ready-made crust instead.

TO START Get all your ingredients and equipment ready. Turn your oven to 375°. Fill and boil the kettle. Put a large frying pan on a high heat. Put the standard blade attachment into the food processor.

PASTA Trim the scallions, carrot, and celery. Roughly chop all the vegetables, then blitz in the food processor with the chiles (stalks removed). Add the sausages, 1 heaping teaspoon of fennel seeds, and 1 teaspoon of oregano. Keep pulsing until well mixed, then spoon this mixture into the hot frying pan with a lug of olive oil, breaking it up and stirring as you go. Keep checking on it and stirring while you get on with other jobs. Put a large deep saucepan on a low heat and fill with boiled water. Fill and reboil the kettle.

TARTS Put the 6 pie shells on a baking sheet. Make a frangipane mixture by cracking the egg into a mixing bowl and adding 1 cup almond meal, 7 tablespoons of butter, and ½ cup superfine sugar. Grate over the zest of ½ an orange and add 1 tablespoon of vanilla paste or extract. Use a spoon to mix everything together.

Spoon a small teaspoon of jam into each pastry base. Top with a heaping teaspoon of frangipane, add another small teaspoon of jam, then finally another heaping teaspoon of frangipane. Put the pan in the oven on the middle shelf and set the timer for 18 minutes exactly.

Note: If using a 9-inch crust, lower the oven temperature to 350° and cook the tart for 25 to 30 minutes.

PASTA Top up the saucepan with more boiled water if needed. Season well, then add the penne and cook following the package instructions, with the lid askew.

SALAD Trim off the bases of the endives, then pull apart all the leaves and quarter the heart. Scatter over a platter, then sprinkle the arugula and watercress on top and toss quickly with your hands.

PASTA Crush 4 unpeeled cloves garlic into the sausage mixture and stir in ¼ cup of balsamic vinegar and the canned tomatoes. Add a little of the starchy cooking water from the pasta to loosen, if needed.

SALAD Peel or shave some of the Parmesan over the endive salad and take it to the table with a bottle of extra virgin olive oil, salt, pepper, and lemon wedges for dressing right before eating.

PASTA Drain the pasta, reserving about a wineglass worth of the cooking water. Tip the pasta into the pan of sauce and give it a gentle stir, adding enough of the cooking water to bring it to a silky consistency. Taste, correct the seasoning, then tip into a large serving bowl and take straight to the table with the rest of the Parmesan for grating over. Scatter over a few basil leaves.

TARTS When the little tarts are golden and cooked, turn the oven off and take them out. Serve them warm, with a dollop of crème fraîche on the side.

CAULIFLOWER MACARONI

SERVES 6

BELGIAN ENDIVE SALAD WITH INSANE DRESSING
LOVELY STEWED FRUIT

CAULIFLOWER MACARONI

8 slices pancetta
1 large head of cauliflower
1 pound dried macaroni (elbows)
9 ounces sharp Cheddar cheese
4 thick slices of country bread
a few sprigs of fresh rosemary
2 cloves garlic
1 cup crème fraîche
Parmesan cheese, to serve

SALAD

2 large heads red endive, or 1 large
  radicchio
2 large heads Belgian endive
a small bunch of fresh basil
1 clove garlic
$\frac{1}{4}$ x 2-ounce can anchovies in oil,
  drained
1 teaspoon Dijon mustard
2 tablespoons natural yogurt
3 tablespoons red wine vinegar
a small handful of capers, drained

SEASONINGS

olive oil
extra virgin olive oil
sea salt & black pepper

STEWED FRUIT

18 ripe plums or a mixture of
  any stone fruit you like, such as
  nectarines or apricots
1 teaspoon vanilla paste or extract
2 heaping tablespoons superfine
  sugar
1 orange
1 cinnamon stick
optional: a good splash of brandy
1 pint good-quality vanilla ice cream

TO START Get all your ingredients and equipment ready. Fill and boil the kettle. Turn the oven on to 425°F. Put the coarse grater attachment into the food processor.

CAULIFLOWER MACARONI Lay the pancetta in a roasting pan (approx. 9 x 13 inches, or large enough to bake the pasta in) and put on the top shelf of the oven. Get rid of any tatty outer leaves from the cauliflower, then trim off the tough base of the stalk and quarter the head. Put in a large saucepan, core downwards, with the pasta, on a high heat. Cover with boiling water, filling and reboiling the kettle if necessary. Season with a good pinch of salt, drizzle over a little olive oil, then stir and cook following the package instructions, with the lid askew.

STEWED FRUIT Halve and stone the plums and put them into another large roasting pan with 1 teaspoon of vanilla paste or extract and 2 heaping tablespoons of superfine sugar. Peel in the zest from $\frac{1}{2}$ the orange, then squeeze in all the juice. Add the cinnamon stick, snapped in half, and stir in a good slug of brandy, if using. Put on the bottom shelf of the oven. They will be perfect after about 15 minutes.

CAULIFLOWER MACARONI Grate the Cheddar in the food processor and tip into a bowl. Fit the standard blade attachment, then get your pancetta out of the oven and blitz in the processor with the bread, rosemary leaves, and a good drizzle of olive oil until you have a coarse breadcrumb consistency.

Put a colander over a large bowl to catch the pasta water, then drain the pasta and cauliflower. Tip into the roasting pan you cooked your pancetta in, and put over a low heat. Add 1⅔ cups of the reserved pasta water from the bowl. Crush in the 2 unpeeled cloves of garlic and mix in the crème fraîche and grated Cheddar, gently breaking up the cauliflower with tongs or a potato masher. Have a taste

and correct the seasoning. It should be nice and loose; if not, add another splash of the pasta water.

Spread out evenly and scatter over the breadcrumbs. Put on the top shelf of the oven for about 8 minutes, or until golden and bubbling.

STEWED FRUIT If the plums look soft and juicy, take them out of the oven and set aside. If not, leave them in a little longer.

SALAD Trim the bases of the endives and pull the leaves apart over a serving platter. Quickly pick the basil leaves and scatter the small ones all over the salad. Put a small frying pan on a medium to low heat.

Put the bigger basil leaves into a blender. Crush in the unpeeled garlic clove, then add a good pinch of salt & pepper, $\frac{1}{4}$ the can of anchovies plus a little of their oil, 1 teaspoon of mustard, 2 tablespoons of yogurt, 3 tablespoons of red wine vinegar and about the same amount of extra virgin olive oil. Add a small splash of water and whiz until smooth.

Add a splash of olive oil and the capers to the hot frying pan. Fry for a few minutes until crispy. Taste the dressing to check for acidity, then pour into a jug. Sprinkle the crispy capers all over the leaves and take to the table with the jug of dressing. You won't need all the dressing – keep any extra in the refrigerator for another day.

TO SERVE When the cauliflower macaroni is golden and bubbling, take it to the table and shave over some Parmesan. If the fruit is still in the oven, take it out and put it to one side. Take the ice cream out of the freezer to soften. When ready, serve the fruit in small glasses, layered up with vanilla ice cream.

TRAPANI-STYLE RIGATONI

GRIDDLED ENDIVE SALAD

ARUGULA & PARMESAN SALAD

LIMONCELLO KINDA TRIFLE

SERVES 6

CIABATTA
1 ciabatta loaf
1 heaping teaspoon dried thyme

PASTA
1 pound dried rigatoni
2 ounces Parmesan cheese
¾ cup whole skinned almonds
2 cloves garlic
1–2 fresh red chiles
2 large bunches of fresh basil
4 anchovy fillets in oil
3 cups cherry or grape tomatoes, red
  and yellow if possible

ENDIVE SALAD
2 heads red endive, or 1 large radicchio
2 heads Belgian endive
balsamic vinegar
a few sprigs of fresh rosemary
½ clove garlic

ARUGULA SALAD
1 x 5-ounce package prewashed
  arugula
2 ounces Parmesan cheese
½ lemon

SEASONINGS
olive oil
extra virgin olive oil
sea salt & black pepper

TRIFLE
3 oranges
⅓ cup limoncello
4 ounces (about 12) ladyfingers
  (savoiardi)
1 cup mascarpone
2 heaping tablespoons confectioners'
  sugar, plus extra for dusting
½ cup reduced-fat milk
1 lemon
1 teaspoon vanilla paste or extract
1 cup raspberries, or other
  seasonal fruit
1 x 4-ounce bar of good-quality
  bittersweet chocolate (62% cocoa
  solids, or higher), for shaving over

TO START Get all your ingredients and equipment ready. Fill and boil the kettle. Turn the oven on to 350°F. Put a couple of inches of hot water into a large saucepan on a medium heat. Put a grill pan on a high heat. Put the standard blade attachment into the food processor.

CIABATTA Drizzle the ciabatta with olive oil and sprinkle over the dried thyme and a good pinch of salt. Put in the oven.

TRIFLE Squeeze the juice from 3 oranges into an appropriately sized serving dish. Stir in the limoncello and taste to check the balance of sweetness and alcohol, adjusting if necessary. Cover the base of the dish with a layer of ladyfingers. Put the mascarpone and confectioners' sugar into a separate bowl with the milk. Finely grate over the zest of the lemon, then squeeze in the juice from one half. Add the vanilla paste or extract to the bowl and whisk well. Spread this mixture all over the ladyfingers, then scatter over the raspberries and finely scrape over a little dark chocolate. Put into the refrigerator.

ENDIVE SALAD Trim the endives and halve each one lengthways. Lay them flat side down on the grill pan. Turn every few minutes and take the pan off the heat once nicely charred on both sides.

PASTA Add the pasta and boiling water to the large saucepan, turn up to a high heat, and cook following the package instructions, with the lid askew. Fill and reboil the kettle for topping up, if needed.

ARUGULA SALAD Put the arugula into a bowl. Use a vegetable peeler to shave the Parmesan over. In a small pitcher, mix 3 tablespoons of extra virgin olive oil with the juice of ½ lemon, then season to taste. Take the salad and dressing to the table.

PASTA Put the Parmesan, ¾ cup almonds, 2 peeled cloves garlic, and 1 or 2 chiles (stalks removed) into a food processor and whiz until fine. While the processor is still running, add 1½ bunches of basil, 4 anchovies, and two-thirds of the cherry tomatoes. Whiz to a paste, then add a lug or 2 of extra virgin olive oil. Taste and season if needed, then put aside. Halve or quarter the remaining tomatoes, then put aside. By now the pasta should be perfectly cooked, so drain, reserving some of the cooking water, and return it to the hot pan. Add the paste, mixing well to coat the pasta. Add a splash of water to make it silky and loose.

ENDIVE SALAD Move the endives to the board. Roughly chop, then dress with a couple of splashes of balsamic vinegar and a couple of lugs of extra virgin olive oil. Season with salt & pepper. Pick and finely chop the rosemary leaves and crush over ½ peeled clove of garlic. Toss together and take to the table.

CIABATTA Remove the bread from the oven, put it on a board, and take to the table.

PASTA Tip the pasta into a large serving bowl, toss quickly, then scatter the reserved cherry tomatoes and basil on top and take to the table.

TRIFLE After dinner, take the dessert out of the refrigerator. Sieve over a little confectioners' sugar, then serve. If you're feeling a bit indulgent you can melt the rest of the chocolate in the microwave and drizzle it over the top.

WONKY SUMMER PASTA

SERVES 4

HERBY SALAD
PEAR DROP TARTLETS

PASTA*

2 egg yolks
5 ounces Parmesan cheese, plus
  extra for serving
zest and juice of 2 lemons
a small bunch of fresh basil
1 pound fresh lasagne sheets, thawed
  if frozen

SALAD

8 slices pancetta
1 clove garlic
1 tablespoon fennel seeds

1 x 5-ounce package prewashed
  arugula and/or watercress
a small bunch of fresh mint
a small bunch of fresh tarragon
a large handful of red, green, or
  mixed grapes
2 tablespoons balsamic vinegar
½ lemon

SEASONINGS

olive oil
extra virgin olive oil
sea salt & black pepper

TARTLETS

4 individual ready-to-use pie shells
  (or 1 x 9-inch ready-made shell)
4 soup spoons raspberry jam
1 x 15-ounce can pear halves in
  natural juice
optional: 2 sprigs of fresh lemon
  thyme
½ cup superfine sugar
2 egg whites
1 teaspoon vanilla paste or extract
1 pint good-quality vanilla ice
  cream, to serve

TO START Get all your ingredients and equipment ready. Turn the oven on to 375°F. Fill a large saucepan with hot water, put it on a high heat and cover with a lid. Put the fine grater attachment into the food processor.

TARTLETS Put the pie shells onto a baking sheet and spoon 1 soup spoon of raspberry jam into each one. Slice 4 pear halves and divide between the pastry shells. Scatter a few lemon thyme leaves over each, if using. (If using a 9-inch shell, use all of the pear halves from the can.)

PASTA Carefully separate 2 eggs and put the yolks into a big serving bowl. Put the whites into a small mixing bowl.

TARTLETS Add the superfine sugar and a pinch of salt to the small mixing bowl with the egg whites, turn on the electric whisk, and leave running at full speed until the mixture is glossy and stiff.

PASTA Add 3 tablespoons of extra virgin olive oil and a good pinch of salt & pepper to the bowl of egg yolks. Grate the Parmesan in the processor and tip it into the bowl of egg yolks with the lemon zest and juice. Reserve some of the small basil leaves, then split the rest of the bunch into 2 halves. Pound one half in a pestle & mortar until you have a green paste, and roughly chop the other half. Add both to the bowl. Stir until everything is mixed together, then season with salt & pepper.

TARTLETS The egg whites should be glossy, smooth, and thick by now, so mix in the vanilla paste or extract, then spoon and smooth the meringue over the tartlets so you get lovely peaks. Put into the oven on the middle shelf and set the timer for 6 minutes, or until golden and lovely. (If using a 9-inch shell, lower the oven temperature to 350° and cook the tart for 20 minutes.)

SALAD Put the pancetta into an empty frying pan on a medium heat and add a squashed, unpeeled clove of garlic. Once the slices are golden, turn them over and add the tablespoon of fennel seeds. Meanwhile, put the salad leaves onto a serving platter or into a large bowl. Quickly tear in some mint and tarragon leaves, and add a large handful of whole or halved grapes. When the pancetta is nice and crispy, take the pan off the heat. Toss the salad together and put on a platter. Crumble over the crispy pancetta, and sprinkle the fennel seeds on top.

Make the dressing. Pour ¼ cup of extra virgin olive oil and 2 tablespoons of balsamic vinegar into a small pitcher or screw-top jar. Add a pinch of salt & pepper and squeeze in the juice of ½ lemon, then take to the table with the salad so you can dress it right before tucking in.

PASTA Stack the lasagne sheets on a chopping board and carefully slice them into fairly thin strips – do this in batches. Add to the pan of boiling water with a good pinch of salt. Stir, then put the lid on slightly askew and keep it at a hard boil for just 1½ minutes.

TARTLETS Check on your tartlets and take them out to cool if cooked. Take the ice cream out of the freezer so you can serve it with your tartlets when ready.

PASTA This pasta must be eaten ASAP to be enjoyed properly, so call everyone around the table now. I like to use tongs to move the pasta to the egg mixture, because the cooking water that comes with it is what really makes the sauce incredible. If you find that tricky, just drain the pasta in a colander, but save the water. Toss the pasta and sauce together quickly, then add 2 or 3 more spoonfuls of cooking water to make it silkier if needed. Fresh pasta is constantly sucking up water so make it slightly looser than it needs to be and it will be perfect at the table. Have a taste. Does it need more salt or Parmesan to balance the lemon juice? If so, adjust then sprinkle over the reserved basil leaves and grate over some extra Parmesan. Take to the table, quickly dress the salad, and eat right away.

*This recipe contains undercooked eggs and is not recommended for the elderly, the young, or anyone with a weakened immune system.

SUMMER VEGGIES LASAGNE

SERVES 6–8

TUSCAN TOMATO SALAD
QUICK MANGO FROZEN YOGURT IN BABY CONES

LASAGNE

a bunch of scallions
½ x 2-ounce can anchovies in oil
6 cloves garlic
2 ounces asparagus
4¼ cups frozen peas
2½ cups frozen shelled fava beans,
  or edamame beans
a large bunch of fresh mint
1¼ cups heavy cream
1 lemon
1¼ cups organic vegetable broth
2 cups cottage cheese
12 large sheets (approx. 1¼ pounds)
  fresh lasagne sheets, thawed
  if frozen
Parmesan cheese
a couple of sprigs of fresh thyme

TUSCAN SALAD

½ ciabatta loaf
1 teaspoon fennel seeds
a few sprigs of oregano or rosemary
1 tablespoon nonpareil capers
½ x 2-ounce can anchovies in oil
  (drained)
a small bunch of fresh basil
6 roasted red peppers (from a jar)
1 clove garlic
4 vines of cherry tomatoes, red and
  yellow if you can get them
3 large tomatoes
red wine vinegar
Parmesan cheese, to serve

SEASONINGS

olive oil
extra virgin olive oil
sea salt & black pepper

MANGO DESSERT

1 x 16-ounce bag of frozen mango
  chunks
2 tablespoons honey
1 lime
a few sprigs of fresh mint
1 cup plain yogurt
6–8 small ice cream cones
good-quality dark chocolate (62%
  cocoa solids or higher)

TO SERVE

a bottle of chilled white wine

TO START Get all your ingredients and equipment ready. Half-fill and boil the kettle. Put a large frying pan on a high heat. Turn the broiler on to full blast. Put the standard blade attachment into the food processor.

LASAGNE Trim and thinly slice the scallions. Pour the oil from can of anchovies into the frying pan with half the can of anchovies, add the scallions, crush in 6 unpeeled cloves of garlic and toss well. Trim the ends off the asparagus and thinly slice the stems, leaving the tips whole. Set the tips aside and add the stems to the pan with a pinch of salt & pepper. Add a splash of boiled water. Keep stirring so nothing sticks.

TUSCAN SALAD Quickly tear the ciabatta into 1-inch pieces. Put into a roasting pan, drizzle with olive oil, and toss with the fennel seeds, a few sprigs of oregano or rosemary, and a pinch of salt. Mix so the bread is coated, then put under the broiler on the middle shelf for around 10 minutes, or until golden.

LASAGNE Add the peas and fava beans to the pan of asparagus and stir occasionally. Pick and roughly chop the mint leaves and add to the pan with the cream. Finely grate in the zest of ½ lemon.

TUSCAN SALAD Don't forget to check the croutons. Once golden and crisp, tip into a large bowl and set aside.

LASAGNE Roughly mash and squash everything in the flying pan, tasting and adjusting the seasonings if necessary. Cover with broth and bring back to the boil. Add 1 cup cottage cheese to the vegetable mixture. The consistency should be quite creamy and loose. Put a large deep sturdy metal roasting pan (approx. 9 x 13 inches) on a medium heat. Spoon in about a quarter of the veggie mixture, to cover the bottom of the pan. Top with a layer of fresh lasagne sheets and a really good grating of Parmesan. Quickly repeat the layers until the vegetables run out, finishing with lasagne.

Mix a splash of water into the second cup of cottage cheese and spread it all over the top layer of lasagne. Toss the asparagus tips in the empty frying pan with a drizzle of olive oil. Tip onto the lasagne. Push everything down with the back of a spoon to help compact it, and finish with the thyme leaves, a drizzle of olive oil, and a generous grating of Parmesan. Turn the heat up under the pan until bubbling, then place under the broiler on the middle shelf for 8 minutes, or until golden and gorgeous.

TUSCAN SALAD Get a large cutting board and roughly chop and mix 1 tablespoon of capers with ½ the can of anchovies, most of the leaves from the bunch of basil, and 4 of the roasted red peppers. Crush over an unpeeled clove of garlic and add all of the tomatoes and hack everything up. Sweep it all into a large serving bowl, add a splash of red wine vinegar, a good drizzle of extra virgin olive oil, and a good pinch of salt & pepper.

Add the croutons, then tear in the remaining 2 roasted red peppers and scrunch and squeeze everything with your hands. Taste and adjust seasoning as necessary, adding more red wine vinegar if needed. Top with the rest of the basil leaves, then finely grate over a little Parmesan and take to the table.

MANGO DESSERT Whiz the frozen mango chunks in the food processor with 2 tablespoons of honey, the juice of 1 lime, a good pinch of mint leaves, and 1 cup yogurt. Once smooth, pop into the freezer until ready to serve.

TO SERVE Once the lasagne is bubbling and golden on top, take to the table with the Parmesan for grating over. Serve with a bottle of chilled white wine. When you're ready for dessert, get the frozen yogurt out of the freezer, divide between cones, and grate over a little chocolate before tucking in.

SPAGHETTI ALLA PUTTANESCA

CRUNCHY SALAD

GARLIC BREAD

SILKY CHOCOLATE GANACHE

SERVES 4–6

GARLIC BREAD
1 ciabatta loaf
a small bunch of fresh Italian parsley
3–4 cloves garlic

SALAD
2 bulbs fennel
a bunch of radishes
1 lemon

SEASONINGS
olive oil
extra virgin olive oil
sea salt & black pepper

SPAGHETTI
1 pound dried spaghetti
1 x 8-ounce jar of tuna in oil
2 cloves garlic
1 tablespoon capers, drained
1 x 2-ounce can anchovies in oil,
  drained
1–2 fresh red chiles
a small bunch of fresh Italian parsley
8 jarred black olives, pitted
ground cinnamon
3¼ cups passata or 2 x 14-ounce
  cans diced tomatoes
1 lemon

GANACHE
2 x 4-ounce bars of good-quality dark
  chocolate (62% cocoa solids, or
  higher)
a large pat of butter
1¼ cups heavy cream
3 clementines
12 palmiers or other thin cookies,
  for dipping

TO SERVE
a bottle of chilled Valpolicella

TO START Get all your ingredients and equipment ready. Fill and boil the kettle. Turn the oven on to 350°F. Put a large frying pan and a large deep saucepan on a low heat. Put the thick slicer disc attachment into the food processor.

GARLIC BREAD Slice the ciabatta at 1-inch intervals, three-quarters of the way through. Finely chop the bunch of parsley. Scrunch up a large sheet of parchment paper under the tap, then lay it flat. Scatter it with the parsley and a pinch of salt & pepper. Drizzle generously with olive oil, crush 3 or 4 unpeeled cloves of garlic on top, and smear this mixture all over the bread with your hands, pushing it down into the cuts. Wrap it up well, put it into the oven, and check on it every so often.

GANACHE Pour the boiled water into the saucepan for the pasta and put a large heatproof bowl on top (don't let the bowl touch the water). Smash up the chocolate bars in their wrappers, then unwrap and empty into the bowl. Add the butter, cream, and a pinch of salt. Finely grate in the zest of 1 clementine, gently stir, and leave to melt.

SPAGHETTI Lift up the chocolate bowl and add the spaghetti to the water with a pinch of salt and cook following the package instructions. Put the bowl back on top. Keep an eye on it – if it looks like it's bubbling over, reduce the heat a little. Pour the tuna oil into the frying pan, keeping the tuna in the jar. Crush in 2 unpeeled cloves of garlic and add the capers, anchovies, and their oil. Finely chop the chiles and parsley stalks and add them to the pan. Quickly check

your spaghetti and give it a stir. Roughly chop the parsley leaves and put aside. Cook for 2 minutes, stirring well, then add the tuna, breaking it up as you go, and the black olives. Stir in a large pinch of ground cinnamon and the passata or canned tomatoes.

GANACHE Once melted, give the chocolate a good stir and divide between 6 espresso cups. Halve the remaining 2 clementines and arrange them on a board next to the palmiers. Take to the table.

SALAD Trim and quarter the fennel. Trim any leaves from the radishes. Put the fennel and radishes into the food processor and shred. Tip into a large bowl. Squeeze in the juice of a lemon, add 2 lugs of extra virgin olive oil and a pinch of salt & pepper, then toss and scrunch with your hands. Taste and adjust seasoning as necessary, then take to the table.

SPAGHETTI Once the pasta is cooked, drain it and reserve some of the cooking water. Carefully tip the pasta into the pan of sauce. Add most of the reserved parsley, squeeze in the juice of a lemon, drizzle over the extra virgin olive oil, and toss really well. Add some of the cooking water to loosen it if needed. Tip onto a platter, scatter over the remaining parsley and take to the table.

TO SERVE Take the garlic bread straight to the table from the oven and unwrap. Pour the red wine into glasses and let everyone help themselves.

CHEAT'S PIZZA

3 DELISH SALADS

SQUASHED CHERRIES & VANILLA MASCARPONE CREAM

SERVES 4

PIZZA

1½ mugs self-rising flour, plus
  extra for dusting
½ mug of tepid water

TOPPING

1 x 14-ounce can diced tomatoes
a few sprigs of fresh basil
½ clove garlic
red wine vinegar
2 ounces fresh buffalo mozzarella
Parmesan cheese, for grating over
8 slices of salami
1 teaspoon fennel seeds
½ fresh red chile

ARUGULA SALAD

1 x 5-ounce package prewashed
  arugula
½ lemon

TOMATO SALAD

3 cups mixture of interesting
  tomatoes such as cherry, grape,
  plum, and salad, mixture of colors if
  you can get them
½ fresh red chile
a few sprigs of fresh basil
1 tablespoon balsamic vinegar
½ clove of garlic

MOZZARELLA SALAD

6 ounces fresh buffalo mozzarella
¼ cup green pesto (from a jar)
a few sprigs of fresh basil
1 lemon

SEASONINGS

olive oil
extra virgin olive oil
sea salt & black pepper

CHERRY DESSERT

2 good handfuls of ice
12 ounces cherries or other seasonal
  fruit
½ cup mascarpone
¼ cup milk
1 heaped tablespoon confectioners'
  sugar
1 clementine
1 teaspoon vanilla paste or extract
a few palmiers or other thin cookies,
  to serve

TO START Get all your ingredients and equipment ready. Turn the broiler on to full blast. Put a large (12-inch diameter) ovenproof frying pan on a low heat. Put the standard blade attachment into the food processor.

TOMATO SALAD Scrunch the cherry tomatoes into a bowl with your hands. Roughly slice the larger tomatoes and add to the bowl. Finely slice the chile and add, then tear in the larger leaves from a few sprigs of basil. Add 3 tablespoons of extra virgin olive oil, 1 or 2 tablespoons of balsamic vinegar, then season to perfection. Finely grate in ½ a peeled clove of garlic. Mix and take to the table with the smaller basil leaves sprinkled on top.

PIZZA Turn the heat under the frying pan up to high and dust a clean worktop with flour. Put 1½ mugs' worth of flour into a food processor, then half-fill the same mug with tepid water and add to the flour with a lug of olive oil. Whiz until smooth, then tip onto the floured worktop. Sprinkle the top of the dough and the rolling pin with flour (the dough will be quite wet, so be generous with the flour). Roll the dough to a ½-inch thickness. Drizzle olive oil into the pan, then dust the dough with flour again and very lightly fold it over into a half-moon shape. Lightly fold the half-moon in half, then move the dough to the pan and unfold it, pressing it firmly up the sides of the pan. If you don't have a pan this big, don't cook all of the dough at once, halve it and make two pizzas.

TOPPING Put a third of the canned tomatoes into a blender with a few sprigs of basil, ½ peeled clove of garlic, a splash of red wine vinegar, a drizzle of extra virgin olive oil, and a pinch of salt. Whiz until smooth. Pour over the

middle of the pizza base and spread out evenly. Tear ½ ball of mozzarella into small pieces and dot around the base. Finely grate a layer of Parmesan over, then top with the salami slices. I like to bash the fennel seeds in a pestle & mortar and finely chop the chile, then scatter both of them over the pizza. Put the pan under the hot broiler for 4 or 5 minutes, until golden and cooked through.

MOZZARELLA SALAD Tear the mozzarella into chunks and arrange on a large platter. Spoon a little pesto over each chunk. Sprinkle with pepper and pick over the basil leaves. Finely grate over the lemon zest and drizzle with extra virgin olive oil. Take to the table.

ARUGULA SALAD Open the package of arugula and drizzle in extra virgin olive oil, squeeze in the juice of ½ a lemon, and season with salt & pepper. Toss the arugula in the packaging with your hands, then tip into a bowl and take to the table.

PIZZA Remove it from the broiler, transfer it to a wooden board, and scatter over the reserved baby basil leaves. Drizzle over a little extra virgin olive oil and take straight to the table.

CHERRY DESSERT Put a little cold water into a large bowl. Add the ice and cherries. Spoon the mascarpone into a separate bowl, add the milk, and mix with the confectioners' sugar. Finely grate in the zest of the clementine. Add vanilla paste or extract to the bowl. Mix well. Divide the cream between some serving bowls, squash over the cold cherries, then put on the table with some cookies for dipping.

OOZY MUSHROOM RISOTTO

SPINACH SALAD

QUICK LEMON & RASPBERRY CHEESECAKE

SERVES 4

RISOTTO

1 large white onion
1 celery stalk
½ cup dried porcini mushrooms
2 sprigs of fresh rosemary
1½ cups risotto rice
½ glass of white wine
1 organic vegetable or chicken
  bouillon cube
1 pound mixed mushrooms, such as
  chestnut, oyster, shiitake
1 clove garlic
a small bunch of fresh thyme
a large pat of butter
a 2-ounce chunk of Parmesan
  cheese
½ lemon
½ small bunch of fresh
  Italian parsley

SALAD

⅔ cup pine nuts
1 tablespoon balsamic vinegar
½ lemon
4 cups (8 ounces) prewashed baby
  spinach
3 large sprigs of fresh mint
5 sun-dried tomatoes, packed in oil
1 medium cucumber

SEASONINGS

olive oil
extra virgin olive oil
sea salt & black pepper

CHEESECAKE

3 tablespoons butter
½ cup skinned hazelnuts
8 gingersnap cookies
1 lemon
4 heaped teaspoons good-quality
  lemon curd
1 container raspberries (approx.
  5 ounces)
1 cup light or low-fat cream cheese,
  mascarpone cheese, or crème fraîche
1 teaspoon vanilla paste or extract
a splash of milk
1 tablespoon confectioners' sugar
good-quality dark chocolate
  (62% cocoa solids, or higher), for
  grating

TO START Get all your ingredients and equipment ready. Fill and boil the kettle. Put a large high-sided saucepan on a medium heat. Turn the broiler to full blast. Put 4 old-fashioned glasses for the dessert into the freezer. Put the standard blade attachment into the food processor.

RISOTTO Halve and peel the onion, then put into the food processor with the celery and dried porcini and pulse until finely chopped. Drizzle a couple of lugs of oil into the saucepan, then scrape in the veggies and stir regularly.

SALAD Put the pine nuts into a large ovenproof frying pan on a medium heat and toast, tossing occasionally, until lightly golden, then tip into a small bowl and set aside.

RISOTTO Pick and finely chop the rosemary leaves and add to the saucepan with the rice. Stir well for 1 minute, then pour in the white wine and crumble in the bouillon cube, stirring until the wine is absorbed. Season, then add a cup of boiling water and stir in well. Your job now is to get into the habit of coming back to the risotto and adding good slugs of boiling water, or broth if you've got it (you'll probably use about 1 quart in total), every minute or so for around 16 to 18 minutes as you're getting on with other jobs. To make it oozy and lovely, you're going to massage starch out of the rice and stop it from sticking.

Put the large ovenproof frying pan you used for the pine nuts back on a high heat. Rinse the mushrooms in their package if they look dirty. Tear half of them into the risotto pan and the other half into the hot frying pan with a couple of good lugs of extra virgin olive oil and a good pinch of salt & pepper. Crush over 1 unpeeled clove of garlic. Pick the leaves from a few sprigs of thyme into the pan, stir them in, then take off the heat. Pick the remaining thyme leaves into the risotto.

CHEESECAKE Put the butter into a medium frying pan on a high heat. Wrap the hazelnuts and gingersnaps in a clean tea towel and quickly bash with a rolling pin. Turn the heat off under the melted butter, tip in the crushed nuts and cookies, and stir. Finely grate in the lemon zest and mix well. Take the glasses out of the freezer and divide the mixture between them, gently patting it down until firm.

RISOTTO Put the frying pan of mushrooms under the broiler on the top shelf to crisp up. Keep stirring the risotto.

SALAD Put 1 tablespoon of balsamic vinegar, the juice of ½ lemon, 3 tablespoons of extra virgin olive oil, and a good pinch of salt & pepper into a nice large salad bowl with the toasted pine nuts. Season to taste. Grab handfuls of spinach, roughly slice them ½ inch thick, along with some picked mint leaves, and add to the bowl. Roughly chop the sun-dried tomatoes and add. Use a fork to score the cucumber lengthways, then halve and slice ½ inch thick at an angle. Add to the bowl, then take to the table but don't toss until the last minute.

CHEESECAKE Put 1 heaped teaspoon of lemon curd into each glass and top with a few raspberries. Spoon the cream cheese, mascarpone, or crème fraîche into a bowl and add the vanilla paste or extract and a splash of milk. Stir, then add the confectioners' sugar and another splash of milk and mix really well until it looks soft and silky smooth. Divide between the glasses, scrape over a few gratings of dark chocolate, and set aside until you're ready to serve.

RISOTTO Check the mushrooms and remove from the broiler if golden and crispy. Turn off the broiler. The risotto should be oatmeal-like. Stir in the butter, finely grate over most of the Parmesan, and add a good squeeze of lemon juice. Season with salt & pepper and add a splash more water or broth if needed to make it oozy and delicious. Chop the parsley and sprinkle ½ over the risotto and ½ over the crispy mushrooms. Put the lid on the risotto and take to the table with the crispy mushrooms.

TO SERVE Divide the risotto between your bowls, then top with a big pinch of crispy mushrooms. Toss and quickly dress the salad. Finish off with a good grating of Parmesan, and serve.

SPINACH & FETA FILO PIE

CUCUMBER SALAD

TOMATO SALAD

COATED ICE CREAM

SERVES 4–6

SPINACH & FETA PIE

⅔ cup pine nuts
5 eggs
12 ounces feta cheese
2 ounces Cheddar cheese
dried oregano
1 lemon
a pat of butter
1 pound prewashed baby spinach
12 sheets (approx. 10 ounces) phyllo
 pastry, thawed if frozen
cayenne pepper
1 whole nutmeg, for grating

CUCUMBER SALAD

1 English (hothouse) cucumber
10 black olives
2 tablespoons balsamic vinegar
3 scallions
½ lemon
½ fresh red chile
5 or 6 sprigs of fresh mint

TOMATO SALAD

a small bunch of fresh basil
1 clove garlic
white wine vinegar
2 cups mixed cherry or grape tomatoes

optional: a small bunch of fresh
 Greek basil

SEASONINGS

olive oil
extra virgin olive oil
sea salt & black pepper

COATED ICE CREAM

¼ cup coffee beans
½ cup hazelnuts
1 x 4-ounce bar of good-quality dark
 chocolate (62% cocoa solids, or higher)
good-quality vanilla ice cream

TO START Get all your ingredients and equipment ready. Turn the oven on to 400°F. Put a medium (approx. 10-inch diameter) ovenproof frying pan on a medium heat. Put the standard blade attachment in the food processor.

SPINACH & FETA PIE Put the pine nuts into the dry ovenproof frying pan to toast, tossing occasionally. Keep an eye on them. Crack 5 eggs into a mixing bowl and crumble in 12 ounces of feta. Grate in 2 ounces of Cheddar. Add a pinch of pepper, a couple of pinches of dried oregano, zest of 1 lemon, and a lug of olive oil. Once the nuts are light golden, add them to the egg mixture and mix well.

Put the empty frying pan back on the heat, add a little olive oil and a pat of butter, and pile in half of the spinach. Gently push and move it around and add more as it wilts down. Make sure it doesn't catch on the bottom and when there's room, start adding the rest, stirring frequently.

Meanwhile, take the pastry out of the refrigerator. Lay a large sheet of parchment paper, approximately 20 inches long, on the worktop, rub a little olive oil all over it, then scrunch it up and lay it out flat again. Arrange 4 phyllo pastry sheets in a large rectangle, overlapping at the edges, so they almost cover the paper. Rub some olive oil over them. Sprinkle over a good pinch of salt & pepper and a pinch of cayenne. Repeat until you have 3 layers. Don't worry about any cracked bits. Remember to keep stirring the spinach.

Once the spinach is really nice and dense, take the pan off the heat. Add the wilted spinach to the egg mixture and grate in ½ a nutmeg. Mix well. Carefully move the parchment paper and phyllo into the empty frying pan so the edges spill over. Push it down into the sides of the pan, then pour in the egg mixture and spread it out. Fold the phyllo sheets over the top and let them fall where they will (⌘). Put the pan back on a medium heat for a couple of minutes to get the bottom cooking, then put the pan into the oven on the top shelf to cook for 18 to 20 minutes, or until golden and crisp.

CUCUMBER SALAD Run a fork down the length of the cucumber all around it, then halve and quarter it lengthways and cut the quarters across into ½-inch chunks. Put them into a mixing bowl and set aside. Drain 10 black olives, squeeze out their pits, and tear them into another bowl. Pour over 2 tablespoons of balsamic vinegar and push down on the olives so the vinegar starts pulling out their saltiness. Trim and finely slice the scallions, then add to the olives.

Drizzle ¼ cup of extra virgin olive oil and the juice of ½ a lemon into the olive mixture and stir really well. Seed and finely slice ½ a red chile and add to the bowl of cucumber. Pick the leaves from the sprigs of mint, thinly slice them, and add to the cucumber. Pour over the dressing, toss quickly, drizzle over a little more extra virgin olive oil, and take to the table.

SPINACH & FETA PIE Check on the pie.

COATED ICE CREAM Pour the coffee beans into a blender and blitz. Add the hazelnuts and blitz to a powder. While that's going on, really bash the chocolate, still in its wrapper, against the worktop (this works best if it's straight from the refrigerator). Unwrap and add to the blender. Whiz again, then tip into a bowl and put to one side.

TOMATO SALAD Quickly rinse out the blender. Rip the top off the bunch of basil, reserving a few of the smaller leaves, and put into the blender with a pinch of salt & pepper, a peeled clove of garlic, a couple of good lugs of extra virgin olive oil, and a splash of white wine vinegar. Whiz until you have a dark green oil. Taste and adjust the seasoning if needed. Halve or quarter the tomatoes. Pour this dressing over a platter and set the tomatoes on top. Scatter over some Greek basil leaves or smaller basil leaves and a pinch or two of salt, then take to the table and toss right before serving.

TO SERVE Take the ice cream out of the freezer to soften. Take the pie to the table with your beautiful salads and divide up between your guests. After dinner, take the ice cream to the table with the bowl of powdered topping. Roll a scoop of ice cream in the powder to coat, and eat at once. Store any leftover powder in an airtight container and use another time.

TOMATO SOUP

CHUNKY CROUTONS

CRUNCHY VEGGIES & GUACAMOLE

STICKY PRUNE SPONGE DESSERTS

SERVES 4

TOMATO SOUP & CROUTONS

2¼ pounds ripe cherry tomatoes on the
  vine, red and yellow if you can get them
4 large tomatoes
1 fresh red chile
4 cloves garlic
1 ciabatta loaf
2 small red onions
¼ cup balsamic vinegar
a small bunch of fresh basil
a few dollops of crème fraîche or
  sour cream, to serve

SEASONINGS

olive oil
extra virgin olive oil
sea salt & black pepper

GUACAMOLE PLATTER

a handful of heirloom mixed cherry
  tomatoes
1–2 fresh red chiles
a handful of fresh cilantro
2 ripe avocados
2 limes
½ bulb fennel
1 carrot
½ cucumber
3 ounces grissini
  or other breadsticks

PRUNE SPONGE

1¼ cups canned prunes, drained with
  some juice reserved
heaping ¾ cup all-purpose flour
¼ cup dark brown sugar
3 tablespoons unsalted butter, room
  temperature
1 heaped teaspoon ground
  ginger
½ level teaspoon baking soda
1 egg
⅓ cup milk
golden syrup (such as Lyle's), to
  serve
a few dollops of crème fraîche or
  whipped cream, to serve

TO START Get all your ingredients and equipment ready. Turn the oven on to 425°F and put a large saucepan on a low heat. Put the standard blade attachment into the food processor.

TOMATO SOUP Pull the tomatoes off the vines, but leave some of their green tops on. Quarter the larger tomatoes, then put all the tomatoes onto a baking sheet. Drizzle over a good lug of olive oil and season. Halve and seed the red chile and add to the pan. Crush in 4 peeled cloves of garlic. Quickly toss everything, then put on the top shelf of the oven for 12 to 15 minutes.

CROUTONS Get another baking sheet and rip the ciabatta loaf into 8 equal chunks. Add a good lug of olive oil, a pinch of salt, and put on the bottom shelf of the oven.

TOMATO SOUP Peel and roughly chop the onions and put them into the hot saucepan with a lug of olive oil and a good pinch of salt. Turn the heat up to medium and leave to soften, stirring occasionally.

PRUNE SPONGE Get 4 cups that will all fit into your microwave at the same time. Tip the prunes into a bowl, then spoon 1 tablespoon of their syrupy juice into each of the cups. Divide all the prunes between the 4 cups.

TOMATO SOUP Stir ¼ cup of balsamic vinegar into the onions and let it cook away and reduce down.

PRUNE SPONGE Put the flour, sugar, butter, ground ginger, and baking soda into a food processor and whiz. Crack in the egg, then add the milk. Let it whiz until smooth (you may need to scrape round the edge and whiz again), then divide between the cups (they should be two-thirds full) and put to one side.

GUACAMOLE Squeeze a handful of cherry tomatoes onto the biggest board you have, then finely chop up the flesh with 1 to 2 red chiles and a handful of cilantro leaves, including the top part of the stalks.

TOMATO SOUP Take the pan of tomatoes out of the oven and add everything to the pan of onions.

CROUTONS Check them—if they are crisp and golden, turn off the oven, but leave them in there to keep warm.

GUACAMOLE Halve and pit the avocados, then squeeze them over a board so the flesh comes out of the skins. Discard the skins, add a pinch of salt, squeeze over the juice of 2 limes, and chop everything together until fine. Taste and adjust the flavors if needed, then use your knife to sweep everything to one side of the board. Cut the ½ bulb fennel into wedges. Peel the carrot, quarter lengthways, and cut into batons, then do the same with the cucumber. Sprinkle over a pinch of salt, then arrange the vegetables next to the guacamole. Put a handful of grissini into a glass and take them to the table with the board of guacamole.

TOMATO SOUP In 2 batches, carefully pour the vegetables from the saucepan into a blender. Add most of the basil, put the lid on, cover with a tea towel, and whiz to a fairly rustic consistency, pouring the mixture into a large saucepan or serving bowl as you go. Once finished, mix well, season to taste, and top with a dollop of crème fraîche, a few basil leaves, and a drizzle of extra virgin olive oil. Take to the table with a stack of soup bowls and the pan of croutons from the oven.

PRUNE SPONGE Just before serving, pop the desserts into the microwave to cook on full power for 6 minutes.

TO SERVE Put a crouton or two in the bottom of each soup bowl. Ladle the soup on top, then dig in and let everyone help themselves to the guacamole. When the desserts are ready, bring to the table, drizzle over a little golden syrup, top with crème fraîche, and go for it (use a spoon to turn them upside down in the cups and you'll be in for a treat).

CURRY

ROGAN JOSH
FLUFFY RICE
CARROT SALAD
PAPPADAMS
CHAPATTIS
BEER

SERVES 4–6

CURRY

2 onions
1 medium butternut squash
1 small cauliflower
optional: 1 fresh red chile
4 cloves garlic
a bunch of fresh cilantro
½ x 10-ounce Patak's rogan josh
  (medium) curry paste
1 x 15-ounce can chickpeas
  (garbanzo beans)
1 x 5-ounce package prewashed baby
  spinach
2 cups plain yogurt

RICE

1 cup basmati rice
a few whole cloves

CARROT SALAD

a handful of sliced almonds
5 or 6 carrots
1 fresh red chile
a bunch of fresh cilantro
a 1-inch piece of fresh gingerroot
1 lemon

CHAPATTIS

6 chapattis or flatbreads
turmeric, for dusting

LEMON PICKLE

1 lemon
¼ fresh red chile
2 teaspoons mustard seeds
1 level teaspoon turmeric
1 small dried chile

SEASONINGS

olive oil
extra virgin olive oil
sea salt & black pepper

TO SERVE

1 packet of pappadams
cold beer

TO START Get all your ingredients and equipment ready. Fill and boil the kettle. Put a large saucepan on a high heat. Turn the oven on to 350°F. Put the coarse grater attachment into the food processor.

CURRY Peel and slice the onions and add to the large pan with a splash of water and a few good lugs of olive oil. Carefully cut the butternut squash in half across the middle (for speed, I'm only using the seedless neck); wrap up the base and put in the refrigerator for another day. Quarter the neck lengthways, then slice it into ½-inch chunks—no need to peel them (🔪). Add to the pan. Trim the cauliflower and remove the outer leaves. Cut it into bite-sized chunks, and throw them into the pan. If you want some extra heat, slice up the chile and add it now. Crush in the unpeeled garlic. Finely chop the cilantro (stalks and all). Reserve a few leaves for garnish and add the rest to the pan with a couple of generous splashes of boiled water. Add the rogan josh paste and the can of chickpeas, with their juices. Season and stir well, then put a lid on. Cook hard and fast, stirring occasionally.

RICE Put the cup of rice into a medium saucepan with a lug of olive oil and a few cloves, then cover with 2 cups of boiled water (use the same cup you used for the rice). Add a pinch of salt, then put the lid on and boil on a medium heat for 7 minutes. Fill and reboil the kettle.

CHAPATTIS Scrunch up a large sheet of parchment paper under the tap. Flatten it out, then layer the chapattis on top, drizzling each lightly with a little olive oil and a sprinkling of turmeric. Wrap them in the paper and put them on the middle shelf of the oven.

CARROT SALAD Toast the almonds in a small pan on a medium heat, tossing occasionally until golden. Tip into a small bowl. Wash and trim the carrots. Grate them in a food processor, using the coarse grater attachment, with the chile (stalks and seeds removed), the top third of a bunch of cilantro, and a peeled 1-inch piece of ginger. Tip into a serving bowl.

CURRY Check and add a splash of water if it looks a bit dry. Stir, then replace the lid.

RICE By now the 7 minutes should be up, so take the rice off the heat and leave it to sit with the lid on for 7 minutes. This will let it steam and will give you beautiful fluffy nutty rice.

CARROT SALAD Drizzle a lug of extra virgin olive oil over the salad and add a pinch of salt. Finely grate in a little lemon zest, then add a good squeeze of lemon juice. Toss well. Sprinkle over the toasted almonds and half of the reserved cilantro leaves, and take to the table.

CURRY Take the lid off. Do you need to adjust the consistency at this point? If so, you can add a generous splash of boiled water, depending on whether you want it drier or wetter. Or mash up some of the veggies for different textures. Taste and add a pinch of salt, if needed, then add the spinach and stir through.

LEMON PICKLE Cut the lemon into eighths, then seed and finely slice. Finely slice the red chile quarter. Put the small pan you toasted the almonds in back onto a medium to high heat. Add a drizzle of olive oil to the pan and the mustard seeds, turmeric, and the sliced chile. Crumble in the dried chile. When everything starts to sizzle, add the sliced lemon and a pinch of salt, count to ten, then take off the heat and put in a bowl to cool.

TO SERVE Tip 1 cup yogurt into a small bowl. Drizzle over a little extra virgin olive oil and take to the table with the pappadams and the bowl of lemon pickle. Remove the chapattis from the oven and take them straight to the table. Transfer the rice and curry into large serving bowls. Spoon the remaining yogurt over the curry, sprinkle with the rest of the cilantro leaves, and take both bowls to the table. Crack open your beers and go for it!

Note: Patak's curry paste is available online.

GREEN CURRY

CRISPY CHICKEN

KIMCHEE SLAW

RICE NOODLES

SERVES 4

CHICKEN
8 chicken thighs, skin on and bone in
2 tablespoons sesame seeds
2 generous tablespoons honey

KIMCHEE SLAW
a small bunch of radishes
1 red onion
½ Napa cabbage
a small bunch of fresh cilantro
1 fresh red chile
1 fresh green chile
a 1-inch piece of fresh gingerroot
2 limes
Asian sesame oil

CURRY SAUCE
a 1-inch piece of fresh gingerroot
2 fresh red chiles
optional: a few fresh kaffir lime leaves
a bunch of fresh cilantro
4 cloves garlic
1 lemongrass stalk
a small bunch of scallions
Asian sesame oil
1¼ cups organic chicken broth
7 ounces fine green beans
1 x 15-ounce can coconut milk
lime juice
soy sauce

NOODLES
8 ounces rice noodles
Asian sesame oil
1 lime

SEASONINGS
olive oil
sea salt & black pepper

GARNISHES
prawn crackers
sweet red chili sauce
1 lime
½ romaine lettuce
a few sprigs of fresh cilantro

TO START Get all your ingredients and equipment ready. Put 1 large and 1 smaller frying pan on a high heat. Put the thin slicer disc attachment into the food processor.

CHICKEN Tip the chicken thighs into the largest frying pan, skin side down. Drizzle with olive oil, add a pinch of salt & pepper, and leave to cook, turning every minute or so, for 18 to 20 minutes, or until cooked through. Wash your hands.

KIMCHEE SLAW Wash the radishes well. Peel and halve the red onion. Shred the radishes, red onion, and Napa cabbage in the food processor. Tip into a serving bowl. Add the bunch of cilantro and the chiles (stalks removed) to the processor and whiz. Peel and crush in the ginger, then tip into the bowl.

CHICKEN Put some parchment paper on top of the chicken, then put the smaller frying pan on top of that, with something heavy like a pestle & mortar in it to weight it down. The heat from the smaller pan will get the chicken cooking on both sides and make it nice and crispy.

CURRY SAUCE Put the slicer attachment into the food processor. Peel the ginger and put it into the food processor with the chiles (stalks removed), lime leaves, and most of the cilantro. Crush in 4 unpeeled cloves of garlic. Halve the lemongrass and discard the outer leaves, trim the scallions, and add both to the processor. Blitz to a paste, adding a good drizzle of sesame oil and a good few lugs of olive oil as you go.

CHICKEN Move the top pan to a medium heat and get rid of the parchment paper. Carefully drain away the fat and turn the chicken pieces skin side up. Add 2 tablespoons of sesame seeds to the empty frying pan and leave to toast until golden, tossing occasionally, then put into a small bowl and take the pan off the heat.

KIMCHEE SLAW Squeeze in the juice from both limes, and add a pinch of salt and a splash of sesame oil. Really scrunch together with your hands. Taste to check the balance, then put a large saucepan on medium heat.

CHICKEN Carefully drain the fat again, then wipe the pan with paper towels and reduce the heat. Add 2 tablespoons of curry paste from the food processor, toss to coat and glaze the chicken, then turn the chicken over and carry on cooking to make it sticky and delicious. Fill and boil the kettle.

CURRY SAUCE Tip the rest of the curry paste into the hot saucepan and stir in the chicken broth. Trim the green beans and add. Turn up the heat under the saucepan. Shake the can of coconut milk, then add and stir in. Bring to a boil, then turn down and leave to tick away.

NOODLES Put the noodles into the empty frying pan with a pinch of salt and cover with boiled water. Leave for a few minutes and as soon as the noodles are soft enough to eat, quickly drain, then rinse under cold water and return to the frying pan. Drizzle over some sesame oil and a good squeeze of lime juice. Add a pinch of salt and toss.

CHICKEN Check the chicken is cooked through then add 2 tablespoons of honey and toss, flipping the chicken skin side down again.

GARNISHES Pile some prawn crackers on a serving board with a good pool of sweet red chili sauce. Cut the lime into wedges, put some on the side, and squeeze one of them over. Pull off the lettuce leaves, wash, and spin dry. Put into a bowl and add the cilantro. Take to the table.

CURRY SAUCE Taste and correct the seasoning with lime juice and soy sauce, cook for another minute or so if you want a thicker sauce, then take straight to the table.

TO SERVE Divide the noodles between 4 bowls. Put the chicken on a platter and let everyone layer up noodles, chicken, kimchee slaw, and sauce. Finish with a pinch of toasted sesame seeds.

CHICKEN PIE

FRENCH-STYLE PEAS

SWEET CARROT SMASH

BERRIES, SHORTBREAD, & CHANTILLY CREAM

SERVES 6

CHICKEN PIE

4 x 6-ounce skinless chicken breasts
a pat of butter
a bunch of scallions
6 ounces button mushrooms
1 heaping tablespoon all-purpose
  flour, plus extra for dusting
2 teaspoons English mustard
1 generous tablespoon crème fraîche
  or heavy cream
1¼ cups organic chicken broth
a few sprigs of fresh thyme
⅓ of a nutmeg, for grating
1 large sheet all-butter puff pastry
  (from a 14-ounce package), thawed
  if frozen
1 egg

SMASH

1½ pounds carrots
a few sprigs of fresh thyme

PEAS

1 heart of romaine lettuce
a pat of butter
1 tablespoon flour
1¼ cups organic chicken broth
a few sprigs of fresh mint
4 cups frozen peas
½ lemon

SEASONINGS

olive oil
extra virgin olive oil
sea salt & black pepper

BERRIES & CREAM

1 pound mixed berries, such as
  blueberries, raspberries, or
  strawberries
elderflower cordial (optional)
½ lemon
2 sprigs of fresh mint
a few Scottish shortbread biscuits,
  to serve
⅔ cup heavy cream
1 heaped tablespoon confectioners'
  sugar
1 tablespoon vanilla paste or extract

TO START Get all your ingredients and equipment ready. Turn the oven on to 400°F. Fill and boil the kettle. Put a large wide frying pan on a medium heat and a large saucepan with a lid on a low heat. Put the thick slicer disc attachment into the food processor.

CHICKEN PIE Put the chicken breasts on a plastic board and slice into ½-inch strips. Put a lug of olive oil and a pat of butter into the hot, large, wide pan. Add the chicken and cook for 3 minutes or so. Meanwhile, quickly trim the scallions and wash the mushrooms, then slice together in the food processor. Add to the pan with 1 heaping tablespoon of flour and stir. Add 2 teaspoons of mustard, 1 generous tablespoon of crème fraîche, and 1¼ cups chicken broth and stir well. Pick the thyme leaves and stir into the pan with a few fine gratings of nutmeg and a good pinch of salt & pepper. Leave to simmer.

SMASH Trim the carrots, then quickly slice in the food processor. Add to the saucepan with a lug of extra virgin olive oil, a good pinch of salt & pepper, and a few thyme tips. Just cover with boiled water, then cover with a lid and turn the heat to high. Cook for 15 minutes, or until tender.

CHICKEN PIE Lightly dust a clean surface with flour and unroll the sheet of puff pastry. Use a small knife to lightly crisscross and score it. Take the pan of chicken off the heat. Tip the filling into an ovenproof baking dish slightly smaller than the sheet of pastry (approx. 9 x 13 inches). Cover the filling with the pastry sheet, tucking it in at the edges (like in the picture). Quickly beat the egg, then brush it over the top of the pie. Put into the oven and cook on the top shelf for around 15 minutes, or until golden and gorgeous. Fill and reboil the kettle.

PEAS Return the empty chicken pan to a high heat. Quickly wash the lettuce then slice it in the food processor. Add a pat of butter and 1 tablespoon of flour to the pan, then pour in 1¼ cups chicken broth, tear in the mint leaves, and use a balloon whisk to mix to a smooth and bubbling sauce. Add the peas and sliced lettuce. Squeeze over the juice of ½ lemon, pour in a splash of boiled water, season with salt & pepper, stir, then put the lid on.

BERRIES & CREAM Slice any larger strawberries, if using, then put all the fruit into a large serving dish. Add a little slug of elderflower cordial, if using, and squeeze over the juice of ½ lemon. Mix to coat all the fruit, then pick the mint leaves and tear over. Take to the table with the cookies. Using an electric whisk, mix the heavy cream with the confectioners' sugar and vanilla paste or extract until thick. Put next to the berries on the table.

SMASH Check the carrots are cooked through, then drain and return to the pan. Taste, correct the seasoning, and leave as they are or smash up. Take to the table.

TO SERVE Take the peas to the table, then get the pie out of the oven and tuck in!

Note: Elderflower cordial is available online.

MUSTARD CHICKEN

SERVES 4–6

QUICK DAUPHINOISE
GREENS
BLACK FOREST AFFOGATO

DAUPHINOISE

1 red onion
2¼ pounds Yukon Gold potatoes
1 nutmeg
2 cloves garlic
1 cup heavy cream
4 anchovies in oil
Parmesan cheese
2 bay leaves
a very small bunch of fresh thyme

SEASONINGS

olive oil
extra virgin olive oil
sea salt & black pepper

CHICKEN

a few sprigs of fresh rosemary
4 x 6-ounce chicken breasts, skin on
4 teaspoons English mustard
3 baby leeks or 1 large leek
4 cloves garlic
white wine
¼ cup heavy cream
1 heaping teaspoon whole-grain
  mustard

GREENS

8 ounces Swiss chard or other greens
2 x 5-ounce packages prewashed
  baby spinach
1 lemon

AFFOGATO

1 tablespoon instant coffee (or you
  could use 4–6 shots of espresso)
3 teaspoons superfine sugar
4–6 Scottish shortbread cookies
1 x 16-ounce can pitted dark cherries
  (preferably in juice)
1 x 4-ounce bar of good-quality dark
  chocolate (62% cocoa solids, or
  higher)
1 pint good-quality vanilla
  ice cream

TO START Get all your ingredients and equipment ready. Put a medium saucepan and a large ovenproof frying pan on a low heat. Fit the thick slicer disc attachment into the food processor and turn the oven on to 425°F. Fill and boil the kettle.

DAUPHINOISE Peel and halve the red onion. Wash the potatoes, leave their skins on, and slice in the food processor with the onion. Tip into a large sturdy roasting pan (approx. 9 x 13 inches) and season. Grate over ¼ of the nutmeg, crush in 2 unpeeled cloves of garlic, and pour in 1 cup heavy cream. Tear in the anchovies and finely grate over a large handful of Parmesan. Add the bay leaves, pick the leaves from a few thyme sprigs, and add a good drizzle of olive oil. Use your clean hands to quickly mix and toss everything together, then put the tray over a medium heat. Pour in ⅔ cup of boiled water, cover tightly with aluminum foil, and leave on the heat.

CHICKEN Turn the heat under the frying pan up to medium. Pick and finely chop the leaves from the rosemary sprigs and sprinkle them into the package of chicken. Smear 1 teaspoon of mustard over each breast, then season and drizzle some olive oil over the chicken and into the frying pan. Massage and rub these flavors all over the meat. Put the chicken breasts in the frying pan, skin side down. Wash your hands well. Use a slotted spatula to press down on the chicken to help it cook. It should take around 18 minutes in total.

DAUPHINOISE Give the pan a shake so nothing catches.

GREENS Finely slice the chard stalks so they cook quickly. Wash the leaves. Put the stalks into the saucepan, cover with boiling water, add a good pinch of salt, and put the lid on.

DAUPHINOISE Remove the aluminum foil. Finely grate over a layer of Parmesan. Drizzle the remaining thyme sprigs with oil, scatter on top, and put into the oven on the top shelf to cook for 15 minutes, or until golden brown and bubbling.

CHICKEN Quickly trim the leeks and halve lengthways. Wash them under the cold tap, then thinly slice them and add to one side of the chicken pan.

GREENS Add the chard leaves to the saucepan. Add another splash of boiled water if needed.

CHICKEN Crush 4 unpeeled cloves of garlic into the pan of chicken. Flip the chicken breasts skin side up, then press down on them again. Stir the leeks and add a good slug of white wine.

GREENS Empty the spinach into a colander and pour the greens and the boiling water over the spinach. Add a lug of olive oil to the empty saucepan, squeeze in the juice of 1 lemon, then return all the drained greens to the pan and use tongs to toss and dress in the flavors. Season to taste, then take straight to the table.

CHICKEN Check the chicken is cooked through, then pour ¼ cup of cream into the frying pan. Cover the pan with aluminum foil. Quickly check on the dauphinoise.

AFFOGATO Put 1 tablespoon of instant coffee into a small pitcher with 3 teaspoons of sugar. Half-fill the kettle and boil. Crumble the shortbread cookies into the bottom of 4 espresso cups. Drain the cherries and divide them between the cups. Bash the bar of chocolate up and add a few chunks to each cup. Take the cups to the table.

CHICKEN Turn the heat off. Transfer the chicken breasts to a board and slice into uneven pieces. Stir 1 heaping teaspoon of whole-grain mustard into the sauce, then taste and adjust the seasoning if necessary. Spoon the sauce onto a platter and put the sliced chicken on top. Drizzle over some extra virgin olive oil and take straight to the table.

DAUPHINOISE Take to the table. Get your ice cream out of the freezer to soften for later.

TO SERVE After dinner, stir some boiling water into the pitcher of coffee and sugar. Take to the table with the ice cream and spoon a scoop into each espresso cup. Grate over some chocolate, then pour over just enough hot coffee (or espresso) to start melting the chocolate. So delicious!

TRAY-BAKED CHICKEN

SQUASHED POTATOES

CREAMED SPINACH

STRAWBERRY SLUSHIE

SERVES 4

POTATOES

1½ pounds small red-skinned
  potatoes or baby white potatoes
a few sprigs of fresh rosemary
a couple of fresh bay leaves
6 cloves garlic

SPINACH

a bunch of scallions
3 cloves garlic
a few fresh thyme tips
1 whole nutmeg, for grating
a large pat of butter
1 pound prewashed baby spinach

½ cup heavy cream
1 ounce Parmesan cheese

CHICKEN

dried oregano
sweet paprika
a pat of butter
4 x 6-ounce skinless chicken breasts
1 lemon
2 ounces cherry tomatoes
4 slices smoked bacon
a couple of sprigs of fresh rosemary

SEASONINGS

olive oil
extra virgin olive oil
sea salt & black pepper

DRINK

1 pound strawberries, fresh or frozen
a few sprigs of fresh mint
½ lemon
ice cubes
sugar, to taste

TO START Get all your ingredients and equipment ready. Fill and boil the kettle. Put a medium saucepan on a medium heat, a large frying pan on a low heat, and a large shallow pan on a medium heat. Turn the broiler to full blast.

POTATOES Wash the potatoes, then halve lengthways (or leave whole if using baby white potatoes), and add to the saucepan with a pinch of salt. Cover with boiled water, put the lid on, and boil hard for around 12 to 14 minutes, or until cooked through.

SPINACH Trim and thinly slice the scallions. Add to the large shallow pan with a splash of olive oil. Crush in 3 cloves of unpeeled garlic and add a slug of boiled water. Pick in the leaves from a few sprigs of thyme, finely grate in ¼ of a nutmeg, and add the pat of butter. Leave to tick away for around 3 minutes, stirring occasionally.

CHICKEN Turn the heat under the empty frying pan to high. Get out a large sheet of parchment paper. Sprinkle over a good pinch of dried oregano, salt & pepper, and paprika, then drizzle over some olive oil and add a lug to the hot frying pan now too, along with the pat of butter. Lay the chicken breasts on top of the parchment paper and roll them in the flavors. Add to the hot pan and fry for 4 to 5 minutes, or until golden on both sides. While this is happening, clear away the parchment paper and wash your hands.

SPINACH Pile the spinach into the pan with the scallions and leave to wilt. You may need to do this in batches, but it will wilt quickly. Keep stirring so nothing sticks.

CHICKEN Get out a nice roasting pan, then quarter the lemon and chuck it in the pan along with the tomatoes. Tip in the chicken breasts and any juices from the pan. Use tongs to arrange everything nicely, then lay the bacon on

top of the breasts. Put the frying pan back on a medium heat, add the sprigs of rosemary to the pan, and move them around so that they get coated in the juices. Pop them into the pan, then put the pan under the broiler for at least 14 minutes.

POTATOES Check the potatoes are cooked, then drain and let them steam dry for a minute or two. Add a couple of lugs of olive oil, leaves from a few sprigs of rosemary, and the bay leaves to the empty frying pan. Put the potatoes on top of the herbs in a flat layer, drizzle over some olive oil, and sprinkle over some salt. Crush in 6 unpeeled cloves of garlic, then turn the heat up to high. Get a flat lid from a smaller pan and really press down so you burst and squash the potatoes. Leave to color, then toss after about 3 minutes and squash down again.

SPINACH Stir to help it along. Pour in the cream. Turn down the heat to low. Finely grate in the Parmesan and stir well.

POTATOES Keep checking, squashing, and turning so the potatoes get golden all over.

DRINK Hull the strawberries and add them to the blender with a handful of ice cubes, a few mint leaves, and the juice of ½ lemon. Add enough water to cover and whiz. Meanwhile, half fill a large pitcher with ice. Taste the mixture in the blender and sweeten if necessary. Pour into the pitcher and stir with a wooden spoon. Take to the table.

POTATOES Check and squash down again.

TO SERVE Take the pan of chicken out from under the broiler. Check the breasts are cooked through, then take straight to the table with the pan of spinach. Tip the potatoes onto a platter, take to the table, and tuck in!

KILLER JERK CHICKEN

RICE & BEANS

REFRESHING CHOPPED SALAD

CHARGRILLED CORN

SERVES 4

CHICKEN
4 x 6-ounce chicken breasts, skin on
1 tablespoon honey
a few sprigs of fresh rosemary
a few sprigs of fresh cilantro

CORN
4 large corn cobs, husks
  removed

RICE & BEANS
2 scallions
1 cinnamon stick
1½ cups long-grain rice
2½ cups organic chicken broth
1 x 15-ounce can black beans

JERK SAUCE
4 scallions
a small bunch of fresh thyme
3 fresh bay leaves
ground cloves
ground nutmeg
ground allspice
⅓ cup golden rum
⅓ cup white wine vinegar
1 tablespoon honey
1 Scotch bonnet chile
4 cloves garlic

SEASONINGS
olive oil
extra virgin olive oil
sea salt & black pepper

SALAD
1 red bell pepper
1 head red endive or ½ radicchio
1 romaine lettuce
2 limes
¼ red onion
a small bunch of fresh cilantro
1 cup sprouted cress or alfalfa

YOGURT
1 cup plain yogurt
a few sprigs of fresh cilantro
1 lime

TO SERVE
cold beer

TO START Get all your ingredients and equipment ready. Fill and boil the kettle. Put a large grill pan and a large saucepan on a high heat. Turn the oven on to 425°F.

CHICKEN Put the chicken breasts on a plastic board and halve each one, leaving them joined at the top of the breast. Drizzle with olive oil, sprinkle with salt & pepper, then rub all over both sides of the chicken. Put into the hot grill pan, skin side down, and leave to cook. Clear away the board and wash the knife and your hands.

CORN Put the corn into the saucepan with a good pinch of salt and cover with boiling water. Put the lid on.

JERK SAUCE Trim and roughly chop the scallions and put into the blender with the leaves from most of the bunch of thyme, 3 bay leaves (stalks removed), a large pinch each of ground cloves, nutmeg, and allspice, ⅓ cup each of rum and vinegar, 1 tablespoon of honey, and 2 teaspoons of salt. Remove the stalks and seeds from the Scotch bonnet chile and add chile to the blender, then quickly crush in 4 unpeeled cloves of garlic and blitz with the lid on until you have a really smooth paste. Add a drizzle of extra virgin olive oil to loosen, if needed.

CHICKEN The skin side should be golden now, so turn the chicken over. Pour the jerk sauce into a snug-fitting baking dish and use tongs to lay the chicken on top, skin side up. Drizzle over 1 tablespoon of honey and scatter over a few sprigs of rosemary and the remaining thyme sprigs. Put on the top shelf of the oven and cook for 15 minutes, or until cooked through. Carefully pour away the oil from the grill pan and wipe clean with paper towels, then put back on a high heat.

RICE & BEANS Put a large wide saucepan with a lid on a medium heat. Trim and finely slice the scallions and put in the saucepan with the cinnamon stick, a good lug of olive oil, and a big pinch of salt & pepper. Stir and let soften for a minute or so, then add the rice and chicken broth. Drain and rinse the beans, then add to the pan. Stir gently. Bring to a boil, then reduce to a medium heat. Pop the lid on and leave for 12 minutes.

YOGURT Tip the yogurt into a small serving bowl. Finely chop a few sprigs of cilantro and add to the bowl with a pinch of salt and a good lug of extra virgin olive oil. Finely grate over the zest of ½ the lime and squeeze in the juice. Stir in, then take to the table with the other lime half for squeezing over.

CORN Use tongs to move the corn to the hot grill pan and drizzle over a little olive oil. Cook and turn frequently until charred. Once ready, put on a platter and take to the table.

SALAD Get a very large board that you're happy to serve on. Seed and roughly chop the red bell pepper. Put the red endive and romaine lettuce on top and keep chopping until everything is fairly fine. Make a well in the center. Pour in a few lugs of extra virgin olive oil and squeeze in the juice of 2 limes. Finely grate over the red onion quarter, season to taste, then toss everything together. Tear over the cilantro, snip over the cress, and take to the table.

RICE & BEANS Take the lid off the rice after 12 minutes and give it a stir. All the liquid should have been absorbed. Taste and correct the seasoning if need be, then take to the table.

TO SERVE Take the chicken out of the oven, sprinkle over some cilantro leaves, and take straight to the table. When serving, spoon over the jerk sauce from the bottom of the baking dish. Crack open a few cold bottles of beer and enjoy.

CHICKEN SKEWERS
AMAZING SATAY SAUCE
FIERY NOODLE SALAD
FRUIT & MINT SUGAR

SERVES 4

unsalted raw cashews
...lium-sized red onion
... red chile
...l bunch of fresh cilantro
...blespoons soy sauce

...boon Asian sesame oil
...boon fish sauce
...boon honey

...NISHES
...l hearts of romaine lettuce
...ll bunch of fresh cilantro
...al: 1 fresh red chile
...uce

SEASONINGS
olive oil
extra virgin olive oil
sea salt & black pepper

FRUIT & MINT SUGAR
1 large pineapple
1 heaping cup blueberries or other
  nice fresh berries or soft fruits
a small bunch of fresh mint
3 tablespoons superfine sugar
1 lime
1 cup creamy coconut yogurt

TO START Get all your ingredients and equipment ready. Turn the broiler on to full blast. Lay 4 wooden skewers in a dish of cold water to soak (if they float, use a plate to weight them down). Put the standard blade attachment into the food processor.

SATAY Put the cilantro (stalks and all) into the food processor with the chile (stalk removed), peeled garlic, 3 heaping tablespoons of peanut butter, and a lug of soy sauce. Peel and roughly chop the ginger and add. Finely grate in the zest of both limes, then squeeze in the juice from 1 of them. Add a couple of splashes of water and whiz to a spoonable paste. Season to taste. Spoon half into a nice bowl and drizzle with extra virgin olive oil; put the rest aside.

CHICKEN Line the chicken breasts up on a plastic board, alternating ends, and close together. Gently and carefully push the skewers through the breasts. Slice between the skewers to give you 4 kabobs – see the picture on the opposite page (📷). Thread any stray pieces on the ends of the skewers. To make the chicken crispier you can score it lightly on both sides. Scoop the rest of the satay mix from the processor into a roasting pan, add the chicken skewers, and toss with your hands to coat, rubbing the flavor into the meat. Clear away the board and wash the knife and your hands. Drizzle the chicken with olive oil and season with salt. Put on the top shelf of the oven, under the broiler, for about 8 to 10 minutes on each side, or until golden and cooked through.

GARNISHES Trim the bases off the romaine hearts and get rid of any tatty outer leaves. Pull the rest of the leaves off, halving the cores. Rinse in a colander, spin dry, then take straight to the table. Fill and boil the kettle.

NOODLES Put the noodles in a large bowl, cover with boiling water and a plate, then leave to soak for 6 minutes. Put a medium frying pan on a low heat. Bash the cashew nuts with a rolling pin or against a worktop in a clean kitchen towel. Add to the warm pan and leave to toast, tossing occasionally, and keeping an eye on them as you do other jobs.

Peel the red onion half and put in the processor with the chile (stalk removed) and the stalks from the bunch of cilantro. Pulse until finely chopped, then put into a large serving bowl with 1 or 2 tablespoons of soy sauce and a few lugs of extra virgin olive oil. Squeeze in the juice of 1 lime, and stir in 1 teaspoon each of sesame oil and fish sauce. Mix well, then taste and correct the seasoning. Drain the noodles in a colander, refresh quickly under cold water, drain again, then add to the bowl.

Toss the cashews and turn the heat under them up to high. Add 1 teaspoon of honey, mixing and tossing the nuts in the pan. Once dark golden, tip them into the serving bowl, and add the cilantro leaves. Toss everything together and take to the table with the bowl of satay sauce.

CHICKEN Turn the skewers over, drizzle with a little honey, and put back under the broiler for 8 to 10 minutes.

FRUIT & MINT SUGAR Peel and slice the pineapple and arrange on a large platter with the blueberries. Rip the leaves off the mint and pound in a pestle & mortar till you have a paste. Add the superfine sugar and pound again. Scatter 1 tablespoon of this mint sugar over the pineapple (keep the rest in a small jar in the refrigerator for another time). Halve a lime for squeezing over, then take to the table with the coconut yogurt and a spoon.

GARNISHES Roughly chop the cilantro leaves and finely slice the chile, if using. Put into little side bowls, take both to the table, and put next to the lettuce.

TO SERVE Take the chicken to the table with a bottle of soy sauce and a few wedges of lime for squeezing over. Let everyone build parcels of lettuce, noodles, chicken, a sprinkle of cilantro and chile, and a squeeze of lime.

STUFFED CYPRIOT CHICKEN
PAN-FRIED ASPARAGUS
& VINE TOMATOES
CABBAGE SALAD
ST. CLEMENT'S DRINK
VANILLA ICE CREAM FLOAT

SERVES 4

CHICKEN
a small bunch of fresh Italian parsley
a small bunch of fresh basil
8 jarred sun-dried tomatoes, packed
  in oil
2–3 cloves garlic
4 ounces feta cheese
zest of 1 lemon
4 x 6-ounce chicken breasts, skin on
  and bone in, if possible
4 sprigs of fresh rosemary

VEGGIES
5–6 cloves garlic
8 ounces cherry tomatoes on the vine
a small bunch of fresh herbs, such as
  thyme, rosemary, and bay
1 bunch asparagus
8–10 jarred black olives, pitted

FLATBREADS
1 teaspoon dried oregano
2 cloves garlic
6 flatbreads

CABBAGE SALAD
½ small white cabbage
1 onion
a few sprigs of fresh Italian parsley
a few sprigs of fresh Greek basil or
  basil
½ fresh red chile
2 lemons

SEASONINGS
olive oil
extra virgin olive oil
sea salt & black pepper

DRINK
ice cubes
5–6 sprigs of fresh mint
1 lemon
2 oranges
1 bottle of sparkling water

ICE CREAM FLOAT
1 pint good-quality vanilla ice
  cream
a few teaspoons instant coffee (or
  shots of espresso, if you prefer)
2 sugar cubes
a handful of cantucci cookies

TO START Get all your ingredients and equipment ready. Turn the oven on to 425°F and put 2 large frying pans on a medium heat. Put the thick slicing disc attachment into the food processor.

CHICKEN Pile the parsley, basil, and sun-dried tomatoes, with a drizzle of their oil and a pinch of pepper, onto a chopping board. Crush over 2 or 3 unpeeled cloves of garlic, then finely chop everything together, mixing with the knife as you go. Crumble over the feta, finely grate over the lemon zest and mix again.

VEGGIES Drizzle olive oil into one of the frying pans and squash and add the unpeeled cloves of garlic. Add the tomatoes and the herb sprigs. Reduce to a low heat.

CHICKEN Tear off a big sheet of parchment paper and line up the chicken breasts, skin side down, on top. Use a small knife to carefully fold back the fillets and cut a little pocket in each one, slitting and cutting down until you can open each breast out like a book. Divide the filling from the board into the middle of each chicken breast, pat it down, then fold the chicken back over to cover ( ). Wash your hands.

Add 2 lugs of olive oil to the empty frying pan. Using tongs, lay the chicken skin side down. Scrunch up a sheet of parchment paper under the tap. Flatten out and tuck over the chicken, then leave to cook, shaking the pan every now and again.

FLATBREADS Sprinkle salt & pepper over the messy chopping board, add 1 teaspoon of oregano and a good couple of lugs of olive oil. Crush over 2 unpeeled cloves of garlic. Wipe and roll the flatbreads in these flavors. Scrunch up another large piece of parchment paper under the tap, flatten, then stack the breads up on it and wrap. Put in the oven. Fill and boil the kettle.

VEGGIES Flip the chopping board over and trim the ends of the asparagus, throwing the tips into the pan whole. Mix and toss, then add 8 to 10 black olives.

CABBAGE SALAD Remove the outer leaves of the cabbage half, then quarter and shred in the food processor. Tip into a large bowl. Peel and halve the onion, shred in the processor with the parsley, basil, and chile (stalk removed) and add to the bowl.

Squeeze the juice of 2 lemons into the bowl, add a few lugs of extra virgin olive oil and a good pinch of salt. Toss and scrunch everything with your hands, tasting and adjusting seasoning as necessary. Take to the table.

CHICKEN By now the chicken should be golden underneath, so carefully turn each breast over and add 4 small sprigs of rosemary to the pan. Re-cover with the parchment paper. Put a medium frying pan on top of the chicken to push it down a bit and help it crisp up.

DRINK Fill a large pitcher halfway with ice. Scrunch up the mint sprigs and add to the pitcher along with the juice from the lemon and the oranges. Chuck in 2 orange halves, top up with sparkling water, and stir. Take to the table.

ICE CREAM FLOAT Take the ice cream out of the freezer. Make a pitcher of instant coffee using scant 1 cup of boiled water. Stir in the sugar cubes. Pile the cantucci biscuits on a board with teacups to serve. Put at the end of the table or nearby, with the ice cream.

CHICKEN Transfer the golden chicken to a wooden serving board and slice a chicken breast to check it's cooked through. Pour over the juices from the pan and take to the table so everyone can help themselves.

TO SERVE Take the pan of vegetables and the stack of flatbreads straight to the table.

ICE CREAM FLOAT When ready, put a scoop of ice cream into each teacup and top with a shot of coffee (or espresso) and a cookie. Lovely!

PIRI PIRI CHICKEN
DRESSED POTATOES
ARUGULA SALAD
QUICK PORTUGUESE TARTS

SERVES 4

(with 2 tarts left over)

CHICKEN

4 large chicken thighs, skin on and
  bone in
1 red bell pepper
1 yellow bell pepper
6 sprigs of fresh thyme
cilantro leaves

POTATOES

1 medium potato
2 sweet potatoes
½ lemon
1 fresh red chile
a bunch of fresh cilantro
2 ounces feta cheese

PIRI PIRI SAUCE

1 red onion
4 cloves garlic
1–2 bird's-eye chiles
2 tablespoons sweet smoked paprika
2 lemons
¼ cup white wine vinegar
2 tablespoons Worcestershire sauce
  (such as Lea & Perrins)
a large bunch of fresh basil

SALAD

1 x 5-ounce package of prewashed
  arugula
½ lemon

SEASONINGS

olive oil
extra virgin olive oil
sea salt & black pepper

TARTS (makes 6 tarts)

all-purpose flour, for dusting
1 large sheet all-butter puff pastry
  (14-ounce package), thawed if frozen
ground cinnamon
½ cup crème fraîche or heavy cream
1 egg
1 teaspoon vanilla paste or vanilla
  extract
5 tablespoons superfine sugar
1 orange

TO START Get all your ingredients and equipment ready. Turn the oven on to 400°F. Put a large grill pan on a high heat.

CHICKEN Put the chicken thighs on a plastic cutting board, skin side down, and slash the meat on each one a few times. Drizzle with olive oil and season, then put on the griddle pan that is heating up, skin side down. Cook until golden underneath, then turn over. Wash your hands.

TARTS Dust a clean surface with flour. Unfold the sheet of pastry and cut an 8-inch square from the pastry. Put the trimmings into the refrigerator for another use. Sprinkle over a few good pinches of ground cinnamon, then roll the pastry into a jelly roll shape and cut into 6 rounds. Put these into 6 of the cups in a muffin pan, and use your thumbs to stretch and mold the pastry into the cups (just like in the picture) so the bottom is flat and the pastry comes up to the top. Put on the top shelf of the oven and cook for around 8 to 10 minutes (set the timer), or until lightly golden.

POTATOES Wash the potato and sweet potatoes and halve lengthways. Put them into a large microwave-safe bowl with ½ lemon. Cover with plastic wrap and put into the microwave on full power for 15 minutes.

CHICKEN Turn the chicken over.

TARTS Spoon the crème fraîche into a small bowl. Add the egg, vanilla paste or extract, 1 tablespoon of superfine sugar, and the zest of 1 orange. Mix well.

PIRI PIRI SAUCE Peel and roughly chop the red onion and add to the blender with 4 peeled cloves of garlic. Add the chiles (stalks removed), 2 tablespoons of paprika, the zest of 2 lemons, and juice of 1 lemon. Add ¼ cup of white wine vinegar, 2 tablespoons of Worcestershire sauce, a good pinch of salt & pepper, the large bunch of basil, and a slug of water. Blitz until smooth.

CHICKEN Slice the bell peppers into strips and add to the grill pan. Turn the heat down to medium and keep moving the peppers around.

TARTS Take the muffin pan out of the oven, and use a teaspoon to press the puffed-up pastry back to the sides and make room for the filling. Spoon the crème fraîche mixture into the tart cases, and return to the top shelf of the oven. Set the timer for 8 minutes.

CHICKEN Pour the piri piri sauce into a snug-fitting roasting pan. Lay the bell peppers on top and put aside. Add the chicken to the roasting pan with the sauce. Scatter over the sprigs of thyme, then put the tray into the middle of the oven.

TARTS Put a small saucepan on a high heat. Squeeze in the juice from the zested orange and add ¼ cup of superfine sugar. Stir and keep a good eye on it, but remember caramel can burn badly so don't touch or taste.

POTATOES Finely chop the chile and most of the cilantro on a board, mixing as you go. Add the feta and keep chopping and mixing.

CHICKEN Take the tarts out of the oven and move the chicken up to the top shelf to cook for around 10 minutes, or until cooked through.

TARTS Pour some caramel over each tart (they'll still be wobbly, but that's good). Put aside to set.

SALAD Quickly dress the arugula, still in its package, with extra virgin olive oil, a good pinch of salt & pepper, and the juice of ½ lemon. Tip into a bowl and take to the table.

POTATOES Check the potatoes are cooked through, then use tongs to squeeze over the cooked lemon. Add the cilantro mixture from the chopping board and mix everything together. Season, then take to the table.

TO SERVE Get the pan of chicken out of the oven, sprinkle over a few cilantro leaves, and take straight to the table.

DUCK SALAD

SERVES 4

GIANT CROUTONS
CHEAT'S RICE PUDDING
WITH STEWED FRUIT

DUCK

4 x 7-ounce duck breasts, skin on
Chinese five-spice powder
dried thyme
1 fresh red chile
a small bunch of fresh mint
½ lemon
1 teaspoon honey

CROUTONS

1 ciabatta loaf
a small bunch of fresh rosemary
5 cloves garlic
1 teaspoon fennel seeds

SALAD

1 pomegranate
1 x 5-ounce package prewashed
  watercress or arugula
2 carrots
a small bunch of radishes
1 cup sprouted cress or alfalfa
a small bunch of fresh mint
balsamic vinegar
½ lemon

SEASONINGS

olive oil
extra virgin olive oil
sea salt & black pepper

RICE PUDDING & FRUIT

a handful of sliced almonds
5 heaping tablespoons confectioners'
  sugar
2 oranges
12 ripe plums, mixed colors if you
  can get them
optional: 1 teaspoon vanilla paste or
  extract
2 cups (approx. 16 ounces) good-
  quality store-bought rice
  pudding (from the chilled section)

TO SERVE

a bottle of chilled rosé wine

TO START Get all your ingredients and equipment ready. Put a large (approx. 12-inch) frying pan on a medium heat and a large saucepan on a low heat. Turn the oven on to 400°F.

DUCK Score the fat on the duck breasts in a crisscross fashion, season with salt and a good pinch each of Chinese five-spice and dried thyme, then rub all over with a drizzle of olive oil. Put into the large hot frying pan, fat side down, and cook for around 16 to 18 minutes, turning every few minutes for blushing meat, or until done to your liking. Get a lid slightly smaller than the pan and press down on the breasts to help them get nice and crispy. Leave the lid on.

RICE PUDDING & FRUIT Quickly rinse the almonds in a strainer, then sprinkle over 2 heaping tablespoons of confectioners' sugar. Lay them on a baking sheet and pop on the top shelf of the oven for about 10 minutes to get golden and gorgeous.

CROUTONS Cut the ciabatta into 1-inch-thick slices. Put them into a roasting pan and drizzle over some olive oil. Tear in a few sprigs of rosemary and quickly bash or crush 5 unpeeled cloves of garlic over the bread. Add a good pinch of salt & pepper and the fennel seeds, then toss and mix together and put on the middle shelf of the oven to cook for around 16 minutes.

DUCK Don't forget to keep coming back and turning the duck every few minutes.

RICE PUDDING & FRUIT Quickly peel the zest of 1 orange into strips and add to the large saucepan, squeeze in the juice of both oranges and add 3 heaping tablespoons of confectioners' sugar. Halve and quarter the plums, discarding their pits, then add to the pan with the vanilla paste or extract and mix well. Turn the heat up to high and put the lid on. Leave to cook for around 15 minutes or until soft and delicious. Check on the almonds and move them around with a wooden spoon. Cook for a few more minutes until golden, then take out of the oven and put aside.

SALAD Halve the pomegranate, then hold it cut side down over a large serving bowl and bash the back with a spoon to release the seeds. Pick out and discard any skin or pith. Empty the watercress or arugula on top. Top and tail the carrots and peel them in. Halve or slice the radishes and add to the bowl. Scatter over the cress, then pick and finely chop the mint leaves. Get a small pitcher for the dressing and add a good drizzle of extra virgin olive oil, a good splash of balsamic, a pinch of salt & pepper, and the juice of ½ a lemon. Take to the table, so you can toss and dress the salad at the last minute.

RICE PUDDING & FRUIT If you haven't already done so, take the almonds out of the oven. Stir the fruit gently, put the lid back on, and reduce to a low heat. Tip the cold rice pudding into a large serving bowl or onto a platter.

CROUTONS By now your croutons should be golden and crisp, so take them out of the oven and put aside.

DUCK Once the duck is cooked to your liking (I like mine blushing to medium), get a nice big wooden cutting board. Seed the chile and finely chop with the rest of the mint. Move a little to one side for garnish later, then hit the rest of the mixture with a pinch of salt & pepper, a good drizzle of extra virgin olive oil, the juice of ½ lemon, and 1 teaspoon of honey. Mix and chop everything together on the board. Move the duck breasts to the dressed board with tongs. Cut at an angle into ½-inch slices, then toss everything together. Arrange the croutons around the meat to catch and suck up any tasty juices. Drizzle with extra virgin olive oil, scatter over the reserved chile and mint, and take to the table. Take the stewed fruit off the heat and put aside until ready to serve.

TO SERVE Quickly dress your salad, then let everyone help themselves. Serve with a nice glass of chilled rosé. After dinner, taste the stewed fruit and add more confectioners' sugar if necessary. Spoon over the rice pudding and take to the table with the toasted nuts for sprinkling over.

THAI RED SHRIMP CURRY

JASMINE RICE

CUCUMBER SALAD

PAPAYA PLATTER

SERVES 4

CUCUMBER SALAD
a 1-inch piece of fresh gingerroot
1 tablespoon soy sauce
1 teaspoon Asian sesame oil
1 lime
1 English (hothouse) cucumber
a small handful of fresh cilantro
½ fresh red chile

JASMINE RICE
1 cup basmati rice
2 jasmine tea bags or 1 jasmine
  flower

RED CURRY
2 lemongrass stalks
1 fresh red chile

2 cloves garlic
optional: 4 kaffir lime leaves, fresh,
  dried, or frozen
a bunch of fresh cilantro
2 roasted red peppers, packed in oil
1 heaping teaspoon tomato paste
1 tablespoon fish sauce
2 tablespoons soy sauce
1 teaspoon Asian sesame oil
a 1-inch piece of fresh gingerroot
8 jumbo shrimp, raw, shell-on
7 ounces sugar snap peas
8 ounces cooked salad-size shrimp
1 x 14-ounce can coconut milk
2 limes, to serve
1 bag of prawn crackers, to serve

SEASONINGS
olive oil
extra virgin olive oil
sea salt & black pepper

PAPAYA PLATTER
2 papayas
Greek yogurt
1 lime
2 bananas
a few sprigs of fresh mint
optional: some crisp cookies or
  macaroons, to serve

TO START Get all your ingredients and equipment ready. Turn the oven on to 400°F. Fill and boil the kettle. Put the standard blade attachment into the food processor.

CUCUMBER SALAD Peel and grate 1 inch of fresh gingerroot onto a serving platter and add 1 tablespoon of soy sauce, 3 tablespoons of extra virgin olive oil, and 1 teaspoon of sesame oil. Squeeze in the juice of 1 lime, then check the seasoning. Use a vegetable peeler to peel the cucumber in long ribbons over the platter. Discard the watery cucumber core. Take a small handful of cilantro and finely chop the stalks, putting the leaves aside. Sprinkle the stalks over the cucumber. Finely chop ½ a chile and sprinkle over. Take to the table but don't toss and dress until you're ready to eat.

JASMINE RICE Put a medium saucepan on a medium heat. Add the cup of rice, a pinch of salt, a splash of olive oil, the 2 jasmine teabags or flower, and cover with 2 cups of boiling water (use the same cup you used for the rice). Cover with a lid and cook for 7 minutes, then take off the heat and leave to steam with the lid on for 7 minutes.

RED CURRY Put a large frying pan on a medium heat. Trim the ends and tough outer leaves of the lemongrass stalks, bash up the stalks with the side of a knife, then put into a food processor with 1 fresh red chile (stalk removed), 2 peeled cloves of garlic, 4 lime leaves, a bunch of cilantro, 2 roasted red peppers, 1 heaping teaspoon of tomato paste, 1 tablespoon of fish sauce, 2 tablespoons of soy sauce, and 1 teaspoon of sesame oil. Peel and add 1 inch of fresh gingerroot. Blitz to a paste – you might need to stop and use a spatula

to scrape down the sides so it all gets whizzed up.

Drizzle some olive oil into the hot frying pan and add the shell-on raw shrimp. Let them fry for around 1 minute, then add a tablespoon of the curry paste and fry for 1 more minute. Tip into an ovenproof dish and put into the oven on the top shelf for about 8 to 10 minutes. Put the pan you cooked the shrimp in back over a medium heat. Drizzle in a little olive oil, then add the sugar snap peas followed by the salad-size shrimp. Spoon in the rest of the curry paste, and stir and fry for a minute or two before adding the coconut milk. Stir as it melts down, then leave to simmer on a medium to low heat.

PAPAYA PLATTER Halve the papayas and scoop out their seeds. Fill a small bowl or teacup with Greek yogurt and grate over some lime zest. Halve the bananas lengthways with their skins still on and put on a platter. Halve a lime and squeeze over the whole platter, then tear over a few mint leaves and take to the table with some cookies or macaroons if you like.

TO SERVE Taste the curry and correct the seasoning with a few drops of soy sauce, if needed. Scatter over the reserved cilantro leaves, then take to the table with the dish of shrimp from the oven. Cut the remaining limes into wedges for squeezing over. Put the prawn crackers into a serving bowl, and take to the table. Fluff up the rice with a fork, then take to the table. Toss and dress the cucumber salad. Dish up the rice, ladle over the curry, and divide the large shrimp among everyone.

GRILLED SARDINES

CRISPY HALLOUMI

WATERCRESS SALAD & FIGS

THICK CHOCOLATE MOUSSE

SERVES 4

(makes enough mousse for 8)

SARDINES

8 whole sardines (approx. 3 ounces
  each), scaled and gutted
4 cloves garlic
1 lemon
1 fresh red chile
a small bunch of fresh Italian parsley
1 teaspoon fennel seeds

SALAD

2 tablespoons sliced almonds
1 x 5-ounce package prewashed
  arugula or watercress
2 cups alfalfa sprouts
5 or 6 sprigs of fresh mint
1 pomegranate
1 tablespoon white wine vinegar

HALLOUMI

8 ounces halloumi
2 tablespoons sesame seeds
3 cloves garlic

FIGS

4 figs
honey
2 sprigs of fresh mint
1 lemon

SEASONINGS

olive oil
extra virgin olive oil
sea salt & black pepper

MOUSSE (serves 8)*

2 x 4-ounce bars of good-quality dark
  chocolate (62% cocoa solids, or higher)
a small pat of butter
2 tablespoons superfine sugar
1¼ cups heavy cream
1 teaspoon vanilla paste or extract
2 large eggs
a splash of brandy, Baileys, Grand
  Marnier, or Armagnac
unsweeten cocoa powder, for dusting
1 orange, clementine, or a handful of
  strawberries

TO SERVE

6 whole wheat pita breads
1 lemon
a bottle of chilled rosé wine

TO START Get all your ingredients and equipment ready. Turn the oven on to 425°F. Put a medium saucepan on a medium heat and fill halfway with hot water.

MOUSSE Leave the chocolate bars in their wrappers and smash them against the worktop. Get a large serving bowl and 2 mixing bowls out. Tip the chocolate chunks into a heatproof mixing bowl with the butter, then put over the pan of simmering water and leave to melt, stirring occasionally. Meanwhile, add 2 tablespoons of sugar to the nice serving bowl with 1¼ cups of cream and 1 teaspoon of vanilla paste or extract and whip until silky with soft peaks.

Separate the eggs, adding the yolks to the whipped cream and the whites to the empty mixing bowl. Gently mix through, then put aside. Add a pinch of salt to the whites and whisk really well until stiff. By now the chocolate should be melted, so spoon it into the bowl of whipped cream with a swig of your favorite liqueur and stir through. Gently fold the egg whites through with a spatula, then put into the freezer to set (or in the refrigerator if you're not planning to serve it right away).

SALAD Put a medium frying pan on a medium heat. Add 2 tablespoons of almonds and toast, tossing occasionally until golden, then tip into a small bowl and put the frying pan back on a low heat.

SARDINES Put the sardines into a large roasting pan. Crush over the 4 unpeeled cloves of garlic. Sprinkle over a pinch of salt & pepper. Finely grate over the zest of 1 lemon, then squeeze in all the juice and add the halves to the pan, cut side up. Drizzle over a little olive oil. Finely slice 1 fresh red chile and sprinkle over the top. Finely chop the parsley stalks and scatter them over, along with 1 teaspoon of fennel seeds. Roughly chop the parsley leaves and put aside. Toss with your hands. Put the roasting pan on the top shelf of the oven for around 10 minutes, or until golden and crisp. Wash your hands.

HALLOUMI Cut the halloumi into 8 chunks. Scatter over the sesame seeds and press them into the halloumi. Put a lug of olive oil into the hot frying pan. Squash a few unpeeled cloves of garlic and add to the oil. Turn the heat up to medium. As soon as the garlic starts sizzling, add the halloumi to the pan. Leave to cook for 2 minutes, until golden, then flip over and turn the heat down. Tip any seeds left behind on the board into the pan.

PITAS Splash all the pita breads on both sides with cold water and stack them on the bottom shelf of the oven to warm through.

SALAD Tip the salad leaves and alfalfa onto a platter. Thinly slice the leaves from 5 or 6 sprigs of mint and scatter over, along with the toasted almonds. Halve a pomegranate, then hold 1 half cut side down in your hand and bash the back with a spoon so the seeds fall over the salad. Pour 3 tablespoons of extra virgin olive oil into a small pitcher. Squeeze in the juice from the remaining pomegranate half. Add 1 tablespoon of white wine vinegar, mix, then take to the table with the salad to dress at the last minute.

FIGS Cut a cross in the top of each fig, then pinch the bottoms so they burst open. Pop them onto a little serving board with a small bowl of honey in the center. Pick over the leaves from a couple of sprigs of mint. Drizzle over a little extra virgin olive oil and add a pinch of salt. Cut the lemon into wedges, pop 1 wedge alongside the figs, and take to the table.

TO SERVE Take the pan of sardines to the table with the warm pita breads and the pan of golden halloumi. Scatter the chopped parsley over the halloumi and serve with wedges of lemon for squeezing over and some chilled rosé. When you're ready, take the mousse out of the freezer, quickly dust with cocoa powder, and serve with wedges of orange, clementine, or some strawberries on the side.

* This recipe contains uncooked eggs and is not recommended for the elderly, the young, or anyone with a weakened immune system.

TASTY CRUSTED COD

MY MASHY PEAS

TARTAR SAUCE

WARM GARDEN SALAD

SERVES 6–8

MASHY PEAS

4 medium baking potatoes
1 head broccoli
4 cups frozen peas
a large pat of butter
1–2 soup spoons mint sauce

TARTAR SAUCE

3 cornichons
1 heaping teaspoon small nonpareil
  capers
a small bunch of fresh Italian parsley
½ x 2-ounce can anchovies in oil
1 lemon
¾ cup good-quality mayonnaise
sweet paprika, for dusting

COD

1 teaspoon fennel seeds
2 x 2¼-pounds (or 6 x 6-ounce)
  fillets of cod, skin on, scaled,
  and pin-boned
7-ounce chunk of white crusty bread
4 cloves garlic
½ x 2-ounce can anchovies in oil
½ x 10-ounce jar sun-dried tomatoes
  in oil
a small bunch of fresh basil
½–1 fresh red chile
1½ ounces Parmesan cheese
1 lemon
balsamic vinegar
a couple of sprigs of fresh thyme
a couple of sprigs of fresh rosemary

SEASONINGS

olive oil
extra virgin olive oil
sea salt & black pepper

SALAD

6 slices pancetta
2 cloves garlic
5 tablespoons balsamic vinegar
1 x 5-ounce package prewashed
  watercress
1 x 5-ounce package prewashed
  arugula

TO SERVE

a bottle of chilled white wine

TO START Get all your ingredients and equipment ready. Fill and boil the kettle. Turn the broiler on to full blast. Put a large saucepan on a low heat. Put the standard blade attachment into the food processor.

MASHY PEAS Quickly peel the potatoes (or leave the skins on if you prefer) and chop into 1-inch chunks, add to the saucepan with a pinch of salt, and cover with boiled water. Put a lid on the pan and turn the heat to medium. Trim and discard the bare end of the broccoli stalk. Slice the rest up and add to the potatoes. Break the florets into even-sized pieces and set aside.

COD Put a few good lugs of olive oil into a large roasting pan, sprinkle with salt & pepper and scatter over a teaspoon of fennel seeds. Rub and toss the fish fillets in the flavors, then put skin side down. Drizzle with olive oil, then put under the broiler in the middle of the oven for 5 minutes while you make the topping.

Roughly chop the bread and add to the food processor. Whiz, adding 2 peeled cloves of garlic with a drizzle of oil from the can of anchovies as it's whizzing, then tip the breadcrumb mixture into a bowl.

Put half the can of anchovy fillets into the empty food processor with the drained sun-dried tomatoes, 2 cloves of peeled garlic, basil, chile (stalk removed), and the chunk of Parmesan. Finely grate in the zest from the lemon, then squeeze in the juice. Add a couple of splashes of balsamic vinegar and whiz to a paste. You may need to scrape round the sides between whizzes. Get the fish out of the oven. Spoon and spread this paste over each fillet in a thick, even layer, then scatter over the breadcrumbs. Drizzle a little olive oil over the thyme and rosemary sprigs, then lay on top of the two fillets and put back under the broiler on the middle shelf for 10 minutes, or until golden and crisp.

MASHY PEAS Add the peas and the broccoli florets to the potatoes, and put the lid back on.

SALAD Put a medium frying pan on a medium heat and add the pancetta. Leave to crisp up, tossing occasionally.

TARTAR SAUCE Quickly rinse out the food processor and add 3 cornichons, a heaping teaspoon of capers, a small bunch of fresh parsley, and half the can of anchovies and their oil. Pulse a few times with a drizzle of extra virgin olive oil and the zest and juice of ½ lemon. Whiz until fairly smooth, then transfer to a small bowl and add ¾ cup mayo. Mix well, adding the juice of the rest of the lemon, tasting and adjusting seasonings as necessary. Sprinkle with the sweet paprika, drizzle over a little extra virgin olive oil, and take to the table.

SALAD Once the slices of pancetta are crispy and golden, turn the heat to low, then crush 2 unpeeled cloves of garlic into the frying pan. Take the pan off the heat and add 5 tablespoons of balsamic vinegar. Add a little bit of extra virgin olive oil and shake the pan about. Use a wooden spoon to break the crispy pancetta into pieces in the pan.

MASHY PEAS Drain the veggies, let them steam dry for a few minutes, then tip back into the pan. Add the butter, a good drizzle of extra virgin olive oil, a pinch of salt & pepper, 1 to 2 soupspoons of mint sauce, and roughly mash about ten times. Put in a serving bowl.

COD Check the fish, and when the crust is golden and crisp take it out of the oven and straight to the table along with your bowl of mashy peas.

SALAD At the very last minute tip the salad leaves into the frying pan of warm dressing and toss quickly with your hands. Take to the table in the pan and serve with chilled white wine.

SWEDISH-STYLE FISHCAKES

ROASTED BABY POTATOES

SPROUT SALAD

FRESH ZINGY SALSA

SERVES 4

POTATOES
1 pound baby white potatoes
½ lemon
a small bunch of mixed fresh herbs,
 such as thyme and rosemary

FISHCAKES
2 slices of stale or crusty bread
2 x 5-ounce salmon fillets, skin off
 and pin-boned
1 x 12-ounce haddock fillet, skin off
 and pin-boned
1 x 8-ounce tuna steak
1 lemon
a small bunch of fresh Italian parsley
1 clove garlic

SALSA
1 fresh red chile
1 fresh green chile
4 scallions
4 ripe red or yellow tomatoes
red wine vinegar
½ English (hothouse) cucumber
1 yellow bell pepper
1 red bell pepper
2 limes
a small bunch of fresh basil

SALAD
4 cups alfalfa and/or radish sprouts
1 pack of crispbreads or
 carta di musica (a flat Italian bread)
a small bunch of fresh mint
2 ripe avocados
1 cup sprouted cress or extra alfalfa
1 lemon

SEASONINGS
olive oil
extra virgin olive oil
sea salt & black pepper

TO SERVE
a bottle of chilled white wine

TO START Get all your ingredients and equipment ready. Fill and boil the kettle. Turn the oven on to 425°F. Put the standard blade attachment into the food processor.

POTATOES Pop the potatoes into a large microwave-safe bowl with ½ a lemon and cover with a double layer of plastic wrap. Put into the microwave and cook on full power for 7 to 10 minutes, or until cooked through.

FISHCAKES Whiz the bread in a food processor until fine. Meanwhile, tear off a large sheet of aluminum foil. Put the bread crumbs on top, then put to one side. Add all the fish to the processor. Finely grate in the zest of 1 lemon and rip in the parsley leaves, discarding the stalks. Add a really good pinch of salt & pepper and pulse a few times until coarsely mixed.

POTATOES Quickly pick the leaves from your herbs and finely chop them. Get the potatoes out of the microwave, use a knife to check they are cooked, then carefully remove the plastic wrap. Add the chopped herbs, a good pinch of salt & pepper, and a good lug of olive oil. Mix well. Tip into a heatproof serving dish then put on the top shelf of the oven until golden and crisp.

FISHCAKES Tip the fish mix onto a platter and add 2 heaping tablespoons of the bread crumbs. Scrunch and mix with your clean hands, then divide into 4 patties. If you've got a round biscuit cutter (approx. 4 inches diameter) use that as a mold. If not, use your hands to roll them into 4 balls, then push, squeeze, and pat them into fishcakes. Put on top of the bread crumbs, making sure the cakes are of even thicknesses, then sprinkle the bread crumbs on top to evenly coat them (⬚).

Put a large frying pan on a medium heat and add a good couple of lugs of olive oil. Bash a clove of garlic with the heel of your hand and add to the pan. When the garlic sizzles, use a slotted spatula to carefully transfer the fishcakes to the pan. Cook for about 7 minutes while you make the salsa. Once golden underneath, flip over and cook for another 7 minutes or so until golden on the other side.

SALSA Quickly wash your processor bowl. Seed the chiles and remove the stalks, trim the scallions, and add both to the food processor with the whole tomatoes and a pinch of salt & pepper. Add a swig of red wine vinegar and pulse until very finely chopped. Have a taste and adjust the flavors if needed, and when you're happy pour onto a platter.

Halve the cucumber lengthways then finely chop into smaller pieces. Halve, seed, and finely chop the bell peppers. Mix with the rest of the salsa on the platter and the juice of 2 limes. Pick the baby basil leaves and put aside for garnish, then roughly chop the rest of the leaves and add.

FISHCAKES By now the fishcakes should be lovely and golden brown, so use a slotted spatula to carefully flip them over.

SALAD Scatter the alfalfa over another platter and break over some crispbreads or carta di musica. Thinly slice the mint leaves, discarding the stalks, and scatter over. Halve the avocados and spoon big chunks of the flesh over the platter. Scatter over the cress or extra alfalfa, sprinkle with salt & pepper, and take to the table with a bottle of extra virgin olive oil for drizzling over and 1 lemon, cut in half, for squeezing over.

POTATOES Take the potatoes out of the oven and put them on the table.

FISHCAKES Use a slotted spatula to put the fishcakes on top of the salsa. Sprinkle over the reserved baby basil leaves and a pinch of salt. Take to the table with a bottle of cold white wine.

STICKY PAN-FRIED SCALLOPS

SERVES 4 (with lots of brownies left over)

SWEET CHILI RICE, DRESSED GREENS
QUICK BROWNIES

RICE
1½ cups basmati rice
a small bunch of scallions
3 eggs
1 tablespoon soy sauce
1 tablespoon Asian sesame oil
½ lemon
a small bunch of fresh cilantro
sweet red chili sauce

GREENS
4 baby bok choy
7 ounces broccolini
1 bunch asparagus
½ lime

SCALLOPS
1 pound fresh sea scallops, shelled
  and trimmed
1 lemon
Chinese five-spice powder
Asian sesame oil
optional: ½ fresh red chile
1 clove garlic
honey
2 small pats of butter
a small bunch of fresh cilantro

SEASONINGS
olive oil
extra virgin olive oil
sea salt & black pepper

BROWNIES (serves 12)
2 x 4-ounce bars of good-quality dark
  chocolate (62% cocoa solids, or higher)
1 cup plus 1 tablespoon (2 sticks
  plus 1 tablespoon) unsalted butter,
  at room temperature
1 cup superfine sugar
⅓ cup unsweetened cocoa powder
scant ½ cup self-rising flour
a handful of crystallized ginger
4 eggs
a handful of pecans
a handful of sour dried cherries
1 clementine
crème fraîche to serve

TO START Get all your ingredients and equipment ready. Fill and boil the kettle. Turn the oven on to 375ºF and put a shallow Dutch oven–type pan (approx. 10 inches diameter) on a medium heat. Put the standard blade attachment into the food processor.

RICE Put the rice into the shallow pan with 2 pinches of salt. Cover with 3 cups of boiled water (use the same cup you measured the rice in). Pop a lid on and leave to cook for 7 minutes. Fill and reboil the kettle.

BROWNIES Smash the chocolate and chop the butter into rough chunks, then put both into the food processor and add 1 cup superfine sugar, ⅓ cup cocoa powder, scant ½ cup of self-rising flour, a pinch of salt, and the crystallized ginger. Whiz together. While the processor is running, crack in the eggs. Scrunch up a large piece of parchment paper under a tap. Flatten it, lay it in a sheet pan (approx. 9 x 13 inches), and drizzle it with olive oil, then rub in. Use a spatula to spoon and spread the brownie mixture evenly into the pan, about 1 inch thick. Sprinkle over the pecans and sour cherries and press them down a bit. Finely grate over the zest of the clementine. Put the pan in the oven on the top shelf and cook for 12 to 14 minutes.

SCALLOPS Lay the scallops on a piece of parchment paper. Score crisscrosses on top, only going halfway through. Drizzle over some olive oil, season with salt & pepper, finely grate over some lemon zest and dust with Chinese five-spice powder. Drizzle with sesame oil and toss together to coat in the flavors.

RICE Trim and thinly slice the scallions and put into a mixing bowl. Crack in the eggs, and add 1 tablespoon each of soy sauce and sesame oil and a drizzle of olive oil, then whisk. Take the lid off the rice and use a fork to fluff it up. Pour the egg mixture all over. Squeeze in the juice of ½ a lemon and add a pinch of pepper. Put the lid back

on and turn down to the lowest heat for another 4 to 5 minutes.

SCALLOPS Get a large frying pan on the highest heat.

GREENS Half-fill a large saucepan with boiled water and put it on a medium heat. Halve each bok choy lengthways, trim the broccolini and asparagus, then put in a large colander and cover tightly with aluminum foil. Put over the saucepan of water to steam for a few minutes until tender, then take off the heat.

RICE Thinly slice the leaves and stalks of a small bunch of cilantro and sprinkle over the rice. Drizzle a good lug of sweet red chili sauce on top, then put the lid on and take to the table.

SCALLOPS Put a good lug of olive oil into the empty frying pan. Quickly add the scallops, scored side down. Finely chop the fresh chile, if using. You can jiggle the pan but don't turn the scallops until they've had 2 to 3 minutes, or are golden underneath. Quickly turn them all over and cook for 30 seconds, then crush over 1 unpeeled clove of garlic and sprinkle over the chile. Squeeze in the juice of ½ a lemon and add a tiny drizzle of honey and 2 small pats of butter. Take off the heat, and when melted and sticky put on a plate and sprinkle over the leaves from a small bunch of cilantro.

GREENS Once tender, tip onto a platter. Drizzle with soy sauce and extra virgin olive oil. Squeeze over the juice of ½ a lime. Taste, adjusting if needed.

TO SERVE Take the rice, scallops, and greens to the table. Divide everything between bowls and tuck in. Remove the brownies from the oven to cool while you enjoy the scallops. When ready, serve the warm brownies with a wedge of zested clementine and a dollop of crème fraîche.

SERIOUSLY GOOD

FISH TAGINE

FENNEL & LEMON SALAD

COUSCOUS

ORANGE & MINT TEA

SERVES 4

TAGINE

fennel seeds
1 cinnamon stick
1 small red onion
½ fresh red chile
12 mixed jarred olives, pitted
4 tomatoes
1 small preserved lemon
1 heaped teaspoon ras el hanout
  spice mixture or garam masala
saffron
4 sprigs of fresh cilantro
1 pound mussels, cleaned and
  debearded (ask your fishmonger
  to do this for you)

COUSCOUS

1⅓ cups couscous

MONKFISH

4 x 6-ounce monkfish fillets,
  skin off and pin-boned
2 cloves garlic
fennel seeds
ras el hanout spice mixture or
  garam masala
dried oregano

SALAD

2 bulbs fennel
1 lemon
a small bunch of fresh cilantro

YOGURT

1 cup plain yogurt
1 tablespoon harissa

SEASONINGS

olive oil
extra virgin olive oil
sea salt & black pepper

TEA

a bunch of fresh mint
½ orange
optional: honey
optional: ice cubes

TO START Get all your ingredients and equipment ready. Turn the broiler to full blast. Put a large tagine or Dutch oven–type pan on a medium heat. Put the thin slicer disc attachment into the food processor. Fill and boil the kettle.

TAGINE Put a lug of olive oil, a pinch of fennel seeds, and 1 cinnamon stick into the large pan. On a plastic cutting board, line up the 4 monkfish fillets and trim ½ inch or so off the ends of each fillet so they're all the same size. Put the fillets into a snug-fitting roasting pan or earthenware dish. Roughly chop the trimmings and add to the large pan, stirring frequently. Peel and thinly slice the onion, thinly slice ½ a red chile, and add both to the pan. Tear in the olives, mix well, and leave to cool.

COUSCOUS Put the 1⅓ cups of couscous into a serving dish or pan and season with a pinch of salt & pepper. Just cover with boiling water, drizzle over some extra virgin olive oil, then cover with a lid or plate.

MONKFISH Drizzle olive oil over the fillets in the roasting pan. Crush in 2 unpeeled cloves of garlic. Scatter over a pinch each of fennel seeds, ras el hanout or garam masala, dried oregano, and salt & pepper. Toss, then blast under the hot broiler on the top shelf for 14 minutes, or until cooked through.

TAGINE Roughly chop half the tomatoes, finely chop the rest, and add to the pan. Finely chop 1 small preserved lemon and add to the pan with 1 heaping teaspoon of ras el hanout and a pinch of saffron. Give it a good stir, then pour in 1 cup water. If you've got a tagine, put the lid on. If not, make a mock lid by tearing off a large sheet of aluminum foil (about arm's length) and folding it into a cone shape. There's no right or wrong way. Scrunch the edges together and make sure it fits just inside the pan. Finely chop 4 sprigs of cilantro and add to the pan. Shake the mussels. If any are open, throw them away. Add the mussels to the pan. Put your foil lid on top, sitting it just inside the edges

of the pan. Leave to tick away for around 8 minutes, or until the mussels have opened.

SALAD Trim the base and ends of the fennel bulbs, discarding the outer leaves if necessary and reserving the herb ends if you have them. Halve the bulb, then shred in a food processor, using the thin slicer disc attachment. Squash the lemon with the heel of your hand, then shred in the food processor too. Tip into a large serving bowl. Pick out and discard any end chunks of lemon or fennel. Roughly chop the cilantro leaves, then thinly slice the stalks, discarding the very ends. Put the stalks into a bowl with a good lug of extra virgin olive oil and a pinch of salt & pepper. Mix and toss with your hands. Scatter most of the cilantro leaves over the salad and take to the table.

MONKFISH Check the monkfish. If it's cooked through when you cut into it, turn the broiler off, cover the fish with foil, and leave it in the oven until you're ready to eat. Refill and boil the kettle.

YOGURT Put the yogurt into a bowl. Spoon 1 tablespoon of harissa and a good lug of extra virgin olive oil into the center, then gently swirl it through the yogurt. Sprinkle with a pinch of salt and take to the table.

TEA Rip the mint leaves into a pitcher or teapot. Peel in strips of zest from ½ an orange. Top up with boiling water, sweeten with a little honey if you like, and take to the table. (Or, if you want, serve it cold poured over ice cubes.)

TO SERVE Take the tagine and couscous straight to the table with the monkfish. Remove the foil from the tagine. The mussels should all be open, so discard any that aren't. Scatter over the reserved cilantro leaves. Fluff up the couscous with a fork, have a quick taste to check the seasoning, then serve with some of the lovely monkfish and tagine.

SMOKED SALMON

SERVES 4

POTATO SALAD
BEETS & COTTAGE CHEESE
RYE BREAD & HOMEMADE BUTTER

POTATO SALAD

1 pound red-skinned potatoes,
 skin on
1 lemon
2 sprigs of fresh thyme
a small bunch of fresh dill

SALMON

1 x 5-ounce package prewashed
 watercress
1 pound good-quality smoked salmon
1 lemon
1 heaping tablespoon creamed
 horseradish sauce
1 cup sprouted cress or alfalfa

BUTTER

1¼ cups heavy cream

BEETS

1 x 8-ounce package cooked
 vacuum packed beets
balsamic vinegar
a small handful of fresh Greek basil
 or basil
1 cup cottage cheese
a few sprigs of fresh thyme
1 lemon

SEASONINGS

olive oil
extra virgin olive oil
sea salt & black pepper

TO SERVE

a loaf of rye bread
a bottle of chilled white wine
 or brown ale

TO START Get all your ingredients and equipment ready. Fill and boil the kettle. Put a saucepan with a lid on a medium heat. Put the rye bread on a board and take to the table with a bread knife. Put the beater attachment into the food processor.

POTATO SALAD Wash the potatoes, then roughly quarter them and cut into 1-inch chunks, removing any gnarly bits. Pour boiled water into the saucepan and add a pinch of salt. Add the potatoes, then peel in a few thin strips of lemon zest and add the thyme. Put a lid on and cook for around 10 minutes, or until soft when stabbed with a knife.

SALMON Tip the watercress onto a serving board. Lay the salmon slices over the leaves in rustic waves. Quarter the lemon. Smear 1 heaping tablespoon of creamed horseradish on one end of the board, season with salt & pepper, squeeze over 2 of the lemon wedges, and drizzle with extra virgin olive oil. Take to the table.

BUTTER Pour the heavy cream into the food processor. Leave to beat away – the whole point is to overbeat it.

BEETS Put the beets on a board and cut into erratic chunks. Move them to a serving platter and add 2 splashes of good balsamic vinegar, a good drizzle of extra virgin olive oil, and a pinch of salt & pepper. Quickly pick the Greek basil leaves and sprinkle most of them over. Toss and mix to dress, tasting and adjusting seasonings as necessary.

BUTTER By now the cream should be thick and coming together into one big clump. When ready, it will look like butter and the sound coming from the food processor will change. Put it into a strainer over the sink, then use your clean hands to quickly scrunch and shape it so that any excess water drains away. Put it on some parchment paper; try not to handle it too much or it will melt. Sprinkle over a pinch of salt, then put it beside the bread.

BEETS Measure the cottage cheese and drizzle a little extra virgin olive oil straight into the cup. Rip over the thyme tips and add a pinch of salt & pepper. Finely grate in the zest of ½ lemon and stir. Arrange the beets on a platter, dollop over the flavored cottage cheese, sprinkle over some pepper, drizzle with extra virgin olive oil, and scatter with the remaining Greek basil leaves. Take to the table.

POTATO SALAD Drain the potatoes and leave them to steam dry for 2 minutes while you finely chop the dill. Tip the potatoes into a bowl and add the dill and a pat of your homemade butter, plus a good drizzle of extra virgin olive oil, a pinch of salt & pepper, and the juice of ½ lemon. Toss and take to the table.

TO SERVE Snip the cress on top of the salmon. Serve with chilled white wine or brown ale and any leftover wedges of lemon.

FINNAN HADDIE

CORN CHOWDER

SPICED SHRIMP

RAINBOW SALAD

RASPBERRY &

ELDERFLOWER SLUSHIE

SERVES 4

CHOWDER
4 slices of smoked bacon
a small bunch of scallions
8 ounces red-skinned potatoes
4 corn cobs
12 ounces finnan haddie (or haddock)
  skin off and pin-boned
3 fresh bay leaves
3 sprigs of fresh thyme
1 quart organic chicken broth
⅔ cup heavy cream
8 ounces cooked salad-size shrimp
½ x 10-ounce box large matzo
  crackers or plain crackers (look in
  your supermarket)

SPICED SHRIMP
8 jumbo raw shrimp, shells on
a pat of butter
a few sprigs of fresh thyme
1 teaspoon cayenne pepper
ground cinnamon
4 cloves garlic
½ fresh red chile
½ lemon

SEASONINGS
olive oil
extra virgin olive oil
sea salt & pepper

SALAD
½ fresh red chile
1 clove garlic
a small bunch of fresh tarragon
2 tablespoons red wine vinegar
3 tablespoons low-fat plain yogurt
1 large zucchini
2 carrots
1 fresh red or golden beet
1 cup sprouted cress or alfalfa

BERRY SLUSHIE
ice cubes
2 sprigs of fresh mint
elderflower cordial
1¼ cups raspberries
4 cups club soda

TO START Get all your ingredients and equipment ready. Fit the coarse grater attachment into the food processor. Put a large deep saucepan on a high heat. Turn the broiler to full blast.

CHOWDER Thinly slice the bacon and put it into the saucepan with a good lug of olive oil. Stir until golden. Trim and finely slice the scallions, add to the pan, and stir. Wash the potatoes and chop into 1-inch chunks. Add to the pan and mix well. Keep an eye on the pan, stirring often. Meanwhile, put a clean tea towel over a board and ruffle up the edges to catch the corn. Hold a corn cob upright on the board and run a knife gently down to the base of the kernels, all the way round. Repeat with the rest of the cobs, discarding the cores. Tip the kernels directly from the tea towel into the pan. Add the finnan haddie to the pan with 3 bay leaves and the leaves from 3 sprigs of thyme. Cover with the chicken broth, then put the lid on and cook for 12 minutes.

SPICED SHRIMP Put the jumbo shrimp into an ovenproof pan with a few lugs of olive oil, a pat of butter, a pinch of salt & pepper, a few sprigs of thyme, 1 level teaspoon of cayenne pepper, and a small pinch of cinnamon. Crush in 4 unpeeled cloves of garlic, then seed ½ chile, slice and add to the pan with ½ lemon. Toss and mix well, then put under the broiler on the top shelf for 8 to 10 minutes, or until dark pink and golden on the tips. Once ready, take out of the oven and leave to sit until ready to serve.

SALAD To make the dressing put ½ a chile, 1 peeled clove of garlic, a small bunch of tarragon, a pinch of salt & pepper, 2 tablespoons of red wine vinegar, ⅓ cup of extra virgin olive oil, and 3 tablespoons of low-fat plain yogurt into a blender. Whiz until combined. Have a taste – you want the salt and acid to be slightly over the top, so adjust if needed and whiz again. Pour into a small pitcher and take to the table.

CHOWDER Stir well, then put the lid back on.

SALAD Wash and trim the zucchini and carrots. Quickly peel the beet. Using the coarse grater attachment, grate the vegetables one at a time, all in the food processor. Tip out onto a platter so it looks like a rainbow and scatter cress over the top. Put on the table next to the pitcher of dressing and dress at the last minute.

CHOWDER Add the ⅔ cup heavy cream and the salad-size shrimp to the chowder and stir well. Put the lid back on and turn the heat down to low. Put the crackers in a pile on the table.

BERRY SLUSHIE Rinse the food processor bowl and fit the standard blade attachment. Add 2½ cups or 2 large handfuls of ice cubes and the leaves from 2 sprigs of mint and blitz to a slush. Leave the processor running and add 3 tablespoons of elderflower cordial and the raspberries. Pour in 2 cups club soda and leave to whiz until combined. Taste, adding another little splash of elderflower cordial to sweeten if needed. Pour into a large pitcher, top up with club soda, and stir again right before serving.

CHOWDER Take the saucepan off the heat. You can leave it coarse and chunky, or use a potato masher to mash it up a little bit and make it silky, or purée the lot – it's up to you. I like to roughly mash one side of it, then mix it through.

TO SERVE Take the spiced shrimp to the table with the saucepan of chowder. Roughly break a few crackers into each bowl, ladle the chowder on top, and finish off with a couple of spiced shrimp on the side. Toss the salad in the dressing, taste and season, then tuck in.

Note: Elderflower cordial is available online.

FISH TRAY-BAKE

SERVES 4 (makes enough banoffee pie for 10)

BABY POTATOES, SALSA VERDE
SIMPLE SPINACH SALAD, CHEAT'S BANOFFEE PIE

POTATOES
1 pound baby white potatoes
stalks from a large bunch of fresh
  mint
a squeeze of lemon juice

FISH
4 6-ounce salmon fillets, skin on,
  scaled and pin-boned
8 jumbo shrimp, raw, shells on
a bunch of asparagus
1 lemon
1 fresh red chile
a small bunch of fresh basil
1 x 2-ounce can anchovies in oil
4 cloves garlic
3–4 tomatoes
4 slices pancetta

SALSA VERDE
leaves from ½ bunch of fresh
  mint (from the bunch used for
  the potatoes)
a small bunch of fresh Italian parsley
1 clove garlic
2 tablespoons red wine vinegar
1 heaping teaspoon Dijon mustard
1 heaping teaspoon capers
2 cornichons

SPINACH SALAD
balsamic vinegar
1 lemon
leaves from ½ bunch of fresh mint
  (from the bunch used for the
  potatoes)
2 x 5-ounce packages prewashed
  baby spinach

SEASONINGS
olive oil
extra virgin olive oil
sea salt & black pepper

BANOFFEE PIE (serves 8–10)
¼ heaping cup superfine
  sugar
4 ripe bananas
7 tablespoons reduced-fat milk
1 x 9-inch ready-to-serve shortbread
  pie shell
1¼ cups heavy cream
1 tablespoon Camp coffee, optional
1 x 4-ounce bar good-quality dark
  chocolate (62% cocoa solids, or
  higher), to serve

TO START Get all your ingredients and equipment ready. Make a space in your freezer for a platter big enough to rest the pie shell on. Fill and boil the kettle. Put a saucepan on a high heat and turn the broiler to full blast. Put the standard blade attachment into the food processor.

POTATOES Wash the potatoes and tip them into the saucepan. Rip the leafy tops off the bunch of mint and set aside. Leave the band on the mint, then add the stalks to the saucepan with a pinch of salt. Just cover with boiled water and put the lid on.

BANOFFEE PIE Put a medium frying pan on a high heat. Put ¼ heaping cup superfine sugar into the frying pan and shake the pan to spread it around. Let it melt while you peel 2 of the bananas and blitz them with 7 tablespoons of milk in a blender until you have a smoothie consistency. Carefully tilt the frying pan to help dissolve all the sugar. Once bubbling and golden, pour in the banana mixture. Do not touch anything in the pan – caramel is very hot and can burn badly. Keep stirring constantly, so it doesn't catch, for 1 to 2 minutes, until dark and golden, then pour into the pie shell (🎥). Spoon and spread it around evenly, then carefully slide the pie shell onto a platter and put it into the freezer to cool down for a few minutes.

FISH Lay the salmon fillets and shrimp in a large roasting pan. Snap off the woody ends of the asparagus, then add the spears to the pan with a good pinch of salt & pepper. Quarter a lemon and add it to the pan. Finely chop the chile and add to the pan with the basil leaves. Drizzle over the oil from the can of anchovies and tear in 4 of the fillets. Crush in 4 unpeeled cloves of garlic and drizzle over some olive oil. Roughly chop the tomatoes and add.

Arrange everything nicely in the pan, so the lemons are facing up and the salmon is skin side up. Drape 4 slices of pancetta wherever you like in the pan, then put

under the broiler on the middle shelf for about 10 minutes, or until the pancetta is lovely and crisp and the fish is cooked through.

POTATOES Check the potatoes are cooked through, then turn the heat off and drain them. Discard the mint stalks and tip the potatoes into a serving bowl and dress with a lug of extra virgin olive oil, a squeeze of lemon juice, and a pinch of salt & pepper.

SALSA VERDE Put half of the reserved mint leaves into the food processor. Rip in all the parsley leaves, discarding the stalks. Peel a clove of garlic and add to the processor with the rest of the anchovy fillets, 2 tablespoons of red wine vinegar, 1 heaped teaspoon each of Dijon mustard and capers, the cornichons, and ⅓ cup of extra virgin olive oil. Blitz until combined, then taste and adjust the flavors if needed. Tip into a little bowl and take to the table.

SPINACH SALAD Pour a couple of lugs of extra virgin olive oil into a serving bowl. Add a pinch of salt & pepper, a couple of lugs of balsamic vinegar, and a good squeeze of lemon juice. Thinly slice the last of the mint leaves and add to the bowl. Tip the spinach onto a chopping board, scrunch it up and cut it into ½-inch slices. Pile the spinach on top of the dressing and take to the table to dress at the last minute.

BANOFFEE PIE In a large bowl, whip the heavy cream with a balloon whisk until fairly thick. Lightly fold through 1 tablespoon of Camp coffee, if using, to get a marbled effect. Peel and thinly slice your 2 remaining bananas at an angle. Get your filled base out of the freezer and top with slices of banana. Use a spatula to tip the cream on top of the pie. Scrape over a little dark chocolate (🎥) and pop back into the freezer until ready to serve.

FISH Take the pan straight from the oven to the table. Serve the fish and potatoes with a bottle of chilled white wine.

BLOODY MARY MUSSELS

HERBY SALAD

GORGEOUS RHUBARB MILLEFEUILLE

SERVES 4

MUSSELS

1¼ cups passata or tomato sauce
1 tablespoon Worcestershire sauce
  (such as Lea & Perrins)
1 heaping tablespoon grated
  horseradish (from a jar)
½–1 fresh red chile, to taste
½ head of celery
4 cloves garlic
a splash of port
a good splash of vodka
1 lemon
4½ pounds mussels, cleaned and
  debearded (ask your fishmonger to
  do this for you)
a small bunch of fresh Italian parsley

HERBY SALAD

5 small tomatoes
balsamic vinegar
½ lemon
5 sprigs each of fresh parsley,
  tarragon, dill, mint, and basil
1 x 5-ounce package prewashed
  arugula

SEASONINGS

olive oil
extra virgin olive oil
sea salt & black pepper

RHUBARB MILLEFEUILLE

all-purpose flour, for dusting
1 large sheet all-butter puff pastry
  (from a 14-ounce package), thawed
  if frozen
1 egg
8 ounces rhubarb
2 heaping tablespoons superfine
  sugar
1 orange
a 1-inch piece of fresh gingerroot
1 teaspoon of vanilla paste or extract
½ cup crème fraîche or ½ cup
  heavy cream, lighty whipped
⅔ cup good-quality custard or ½ cup
  heavy cream, lighty whipped

TO SERVE

a loaf of crusty bread
good ale or Belgian beer

TO START Get all your ingredients and equipment ready. Turn the oven on to 375°F. Put a large saucepan with a lid and a smaller saucepan on a medium heat.

RHUBARB MILLEFEUILLE Dust a clean baking sheet with flour. Unroll the sheet of puff pastry and cut in half so you end up with two approx. 10 x 6-inch pieces of pastry. Put one half on the baking sheet, refrigerate the rest for another time. Push down on each corner with your thumb, then score lightly all around the edges, about ½ inch in, to create a border. Lightly run the knife over the pastry in a crisscross pattern. Beat the egg in a little bowl and use a pastry brush to paint it all over the pastry. Put into the oven on a high shelf for around 20 minutes.

Slice the rhubarb about ½ inch thick and put it into the smaller saucepan with 2 heaped tablespoons of superfine sugar. Finely grate over the zest of ½ orange. Peel and finely grate 1-inch piece of ginger and add to the pan. Add a teaspoon of vanilla paste or extract. Put the lid on. Check, stirring occasionally, as you get on with other things.

MUSSELS Put the loaf of bread in the oven on a low shelf to warm through. Pour the passata into a pitcher with 1 tablespoon of Worcestershire sauce and 1 heaping tablespoon of horseradish. Slice ½ chile very thinly (or slice up more if you like it hot) and add to the pitcher. Pull the head of celery apart, wash the heart, then put the delicate yellow leaves on a serving platter. Trim the bottom off the celery stalks, then thinly slice 2 or 3 stalks and add to the pitcher. Crush in 4 unpeeled cloves of garlic and add a slug of port and a generous slug of vodka. Stir really well. Squeeze in the juice of 1 lemon and season with a pinch of salt & pepper.

RHUBARB MILLEFEUILLE The rhubarb should have cooked down now, so turn the heat off and leave it to stand with the lid off so it thickens up.

HERBY SALAD Chop up the tomatoes and remaining celery and put on a serving platter. Scatter over a good pinch of salt & pepper and drizzle over some extra virgin olive oil and a little balsamic vinegar. Squeeze over the juice of ½ lemon.

MUSSELS Pick through your cleaned mussels. If any are open, give them a tap; if they don't close, throw them away. Tip all the good mussels into the hot saucepan and pour in the bloody Mary mixture. Put the lid on, then shake the pan around and leave the mussels to steam open. Turn the heat up to high.

HERBY SALAD Pick the leaves from your herbs and add to the serving platter with the arugula. Add another lug of extra virgin olive oil and balsamic vinegar and season with a pinch of salt & pepper. Take to the table to toss and dress at the last minute.

MUSSELS Check on the mussels and give the saucepan another good shake.

RHUBARB MILLEFEUILLE By now, your puff pastry should be golden and beautiful, so take it out of the oven and use your hands or a slotted spatula to gently press the puffed-up middle back down. Leave to cool for a couple of minutes, then transfer to a serving board or platter. Take the warm bread out of the oven and take to the table.

MUSSELS Once all the mussels have popped open, remove them from the pan with a perforated spoon and put them onto a serving platter, leaving the cooking liquor in the pan over a high heat to thicken and reduce. If any of the mussels are still closed, throw them away. Finely chop the top of the small bunch of parsley. Pour the hot cooking juices all over the mussels. Drizzle with olive oil, scatter over the chopped parsley, and take to the table. Divide between 4 serving bowls and let everyone mop up the juices with hunks of warm bread.

RHUBARB MILLEFEUILLE When ready for dessert, dollop and drizzle most of the crème fraîche and custard all over the pastry base. Top with spoonfuls of the stewed rhubarb, then the rest of the crème fraîche and custard or whipped cream, and take to the table so everyone can have a slice.

BRANZINO &
CRISPY PANCETTA
MASHED SWEET POTATOES
ASIAN GREENS
1-MINUTE BERRY ICE CREAM
SPARKLING LEMON GINGER DRINK

SERVES 4

MASHED SWEET POTATOES
1½ pounds sweet potatoes
2 limes
a small bunch of fresh cilantro
2 tablespoons mango chutney
soy sauce

GREENS
1 fresh red chile
1 clove garlic
soy sauce
1 lime
Asian sesame oil
1 bunch asparagus
1 head of broccoli

BRANZINO
8 slices pancetta
4 x 6-ounce branzino fillets, skin on,
  scaled and pin-boned
1 teaspoon fennel seeds
1 lemon

SEASONINGS
olive oil
extra virgin olive oil
sea salt & black pepper

LEMON GINGER DRINK
ice cubes
1 x 12-ounce can lemon-lime
  soda
a few sprigs of fresh mint
a 1-inch piece of fresh gingerroot
1 bottle of sparkling water

BERRY ICE CREAM
2 x 10-ounce bags mixed frozen
  berries
1 heaping cup fresh blueberries
3–4 tablespoons honey
2 cups plain yogurt
a few sprigs of fresh mint

TO START Get all your ingredients and equipment ready. Fill and boil the kettle. Put a large saucepan with a lid and a large frying pan on a medium heat. Put 4 small glasses in the freezer for the dessert. Put the standard blade attachment into the food processor.

POTATOES Wash the sweet potatoes, trim off any gnarly bits, then stab them a few times with a knife. Put in a large microwave-safe bowl, halve one of the limes and add to the bowl, then cover with a double layer of plastic wrap and microwave on full power for 12 minutes, or until cooked through.

GREENS Seed and finely chop the chile, adding half to a large serving bowl and setting the rest aside. Crush the unpeeled clove of garlic into the bowl and add 2 tablespoons of soy sauce and ¼ to ⅓ cup of extra virgin olive oil. Squeeze in the juice of 1 lime and add a splash of sesame oil. Mix, taste, and adjust the soy sauce if needed. Trim the asparagus stalks. Quarter the head of the broccoli lengthways from the head to the base of the stalk.

BRANZINO Put the pancetta into the frying pan with a drizzle of olive oil. Keep an eye on it, turning when crispy.

DRINK Fill a large pitcher halfway with ice. Add the soda and mint sprigs. Peel and finely grate in 1 inch of ginger. Top up with sparkling water, mix with a wooden spoon, and take to the table.

BRANZINO By now the pancetta should be golden so remove it to a plate, leaving the fat in the pan. Add the fish to the pan, skin side down. Shake the pan and use a spatula to press the fillets flat for a few seconds. Pound 1 teaspoon of fennel seeds in a pestle & mortar and scatter over the fish from a height with a pinch of salt & pepper. Finely grate over the zest of 1 lemon, then cut the lemon into quarters and set aside.

POTATOES Finely chop the cilantro on a large wooden cutting board, setting a few leaves aside for the garnish.

Add the mango chutney, a good splash of soy sauce, a drizzle of extra virgin olive oil, the juice from ½ lime, and the reserved chopped chile. Chop and mix everything together on the board.

GREENS Fill the large saucepan with boiling water and add a large pinch of salt. Add the broccoli and asparagus, making sure they are completely submerged. Put the lid on and turn the heat to high.

BRANZINO Check the fish – once the skin is golden and crispy, turn the heat down to low – but have confidence to let the skin become good and crispy before reducing the heat.

POTATOES Get the sweet potatoes out of the microwave and check they are cooked through, then use tongs to squeeze over the juice from the hot lime halves and discard them. Carefully tip the sweet potatoes on top of the mango chutney mixture and use a knife or masher to chop and mash everything together, including the skins. Season to taste, adding more fresh lime juice if needed.

BRANZINO Take the pan of fish off the heat and flip the fillets over so they gently finish cooking on the flesh side. Return the pancetta to the pan to warm through, then serve the fish and pancetta on top of the board of mashed potatoes. Pop the lemon wedges on the side for squeezing and sprinkle over the reserved cilantro. Take to the table.

GREENS Drain the broccoli and asparagus in a colander, then tip into the serving bowl with the dressing, quickly toss, and take to the table.

BERRY ICE CREAM Get the glasses and the frozen berries out of the freezer. Divide the fresh blueberries between the glasses. Put the honey and yogurt and leaves from the sprigs of mint into the food processor and whiz, then add the frozen berries and whiz again until combined. Spoon the frozen yogurt over the fresh berries and serve. Yum.

ASIAN-STYLE SALMON
NOODLE BROTH
SPROUT SALAD
LYCHEE DESSERT

SERVES 4

SALMON
1-inch piece of fresh gingerroot
2 cloves garlic
1 small red onion
½ fresh red chile
1 tablespoon soy sauce
2 limes
4 x 6-ounce salmon fillets, skin on, scaled and pin-boned
Chinese five-spice powder

SALAD
a large bunch of fresh cilantro
5 cups (14 ounces) washed sprouts or shoots
¾ cup unsalted natural cashew nuts
honey, for drizzling
½ fresh red chile
1 small ripe mango
soy sauce
Asian sesame oil
1 lime or lemon

BROTH
4 scallions
1–2 fresh red chiles
2 cloves garlic
a 1-inch piece of fresh gingerroot
1 teaspoon Chinese five-spice powder
3 teaspoons cornstarch
1 organic chicken bouillon cube
7 ounces sugar snap peas
soy sauce, to taste
8 ounces dried fine Chinese egg noodles

SEASONINGS
olive oil
extra virgin olive oil
sea salt & black pepper

LYCHEE DESSERT
1 cup blueberries
1 x 20-ounce can lychees in syrup
2 x 1.6-ounce packages sesame snap cookies or 3 ounces good quality peanut brittle
1 pint good-quality vanilla ice cream
a sprig of fresh mint

TO START Get all your ingredients and equipment ready. Fill and boil the kettle. Turn the oven on to 480°F.

SALMON Peel a 1-inch piece of fresh gingerroot, 2 cloves of garlic, and a small red onion. Roughly chop and put into a blender with ½ a chile and 1 tablespoon of soy sauce. Squeeze in the juice of 2 limes and blitz to a slurry. Taste to check the balance of sweet and salty, then put into an earthenware dish or a pan that will snugly fit the salmon. Add a couple of lugs of olive oil and put the salmon, skin side up, in the pan. Sprinkle a little five-spice and black pepper over the skin and put into the oven on the top shelf for 18 minutes, or until beautifully cooked through.

SALAD Set aside a few cilantro sprigs for garnish, then pick the leaves off the remainder and put them into a large bowl. Thinly slice the stalks, then add to the bowl with the sprouts or shoots and set aside. Put a large frying pan on a low heat.

BROTH Put a large saucepan on a medium heat. Trim and finely slice 4 scallions, and put into the pan with a good lug of olive oil. Finely slice a chile and add to the pan, then stir and crush in 2 unpeeled cloves of garlic. Peel and finely grate in a 1-inch piece of fresh gingerroot. Mix well.

SALAD Wrap the cashews in a clean tea towel and bash with a rolling pin or against the worktop, then put in the empty frying pan. Add a lug of olive oil, toss, and leave to toast. Toss occasionally until golden.

BROTH Stir 1 teaspoon of five-spice and 3 teaspoons of cornstarch into the pan of scallions. Pour in 3¾ cups of chicken broth and add 7 ounces of sugar snaps. Turn the heat up to high, bring to a boil, then taste and correct the seasoning with soy sauce. Add the noodles and pop the lid on.

SALAD Check the cashews; they should be golden by now, so remove the pan from the heat, add a good drizzle of honey, then toss and set aside.

LYCHEE DESSERT Flip the cutting board over. Cut a small handful of blueberries in half and put into a large bowl with the rest of the whole blueberries. Tip the lychees into the bowl with some of their juices. Stir, then take to the table.

SALAD Finely slice the chile half. Peel the mango, then slice, chunk, and chip away at the flesh (🎥) and add to the salad with the sliced chile. Tip the honey-toasted cashews over the top. Dress with lugs of soy sauce, extra virgin olive oil and sesame oil, and the juice of 1 lime or lemon. Toss with your hands (but be careful in case the cashews are still hot).

LYCHEE DESSERT Wrap the sesame snap cookies or peanut brittle in a clean tea towel and whack them against a worktop to smash them to a powder. Tip out into a small bowl and take to the table with the ice cream.

TO SERVE Take the broth and the salad to the table. Remove the salmon from the oven, sprinkle over the reserved cilantro and take straight to the table. Use tongs to divide the noodles and broth between the bowls. Top each one with a piece of salmon and some spoonfuls of the delicious sauce from the roasting pan.

LYCHEE DESSERT When ready, assemble the desserts by layering up a couple of scoops of ice cream with the fruit in 4 little cups. Drizzle over the juices from the bowl, top each cup with a couple of fresh mint leaves, and scatter over the crushed sesame snap cookies or peanut brittle.

CRISPY SALMON

JAZZED-UP RICE

BABY ZUCCHINI SALAD

GORGEOUS GUACAMOLE

BERRY SPRITZER

SERVES 6

SALMON
2 long bell peppers, red and yellow
a bunch of scallions
2 fresh red chiles
1 x 1¼-pound fillet of salmon, skin on,
   scaled and pin-boned
1 lemon
fennel seeds

RICE
1 cup basmati rice
½ x 16-ounce jar roasted red peppers
a few sprigs of fresh basil
balsamic vinegar

SALAD
1 lemon
a couple of sprigs of fresh mint
1–2 fresh red chiles
14 ounces baby zucchini

SEASONINGS
olive oil
extra virgin olive oil
sea salt & black pepper

GUACAMOLE
4 scallions
a small bunch of fresh cilantro
1 fresh red chile
1 clove garlic

2 limes
2–3 small ripe avocados
1 handful of cherry or grape tomatoes

EXTRAS
6 x 7-inch soft flour
   tortillas
⅔ cup sour cream

SPRITZER
1 heaping cup blueberries,
   blackberries, or strawberries
ice cubes
a few sprigs of fresh mint
a bottle of sparkling water

TO START Get all your ingredients and equipment ready. Fill and boil the kettle. Turn the broiler on to full blast. Put a saucepan on a medium heat. Put the standard blade attachment into the food processor.

SALMON Pour a couple of lugs of olive oil into a large roasting pan. Halve and seed the bell peppers. Slice the peppers and the bunch of scallions into 1-inch pieces. Roughly chop the chiles. Drizzle olive oil over both sides of the salmon, season, and finely grate over some lemon zest. Rub these flavors all over the salmon, then wash your hands. If necessary, halve the salmon so it fits the roasting pan, then lay skin side up and arrange the sliced vegetables all around it. Put under the broiler on the middle shelf and set the timer for 14 minutes.

RICE Put the rice into a medium saucepan with a pinch of salt and cover by ¾ inch with boiling water. Put the lid on, then turn the heat right up and leave to cook for 7 minutes. Once cooked, take off the heat and leave to steam for 7 minutes, still covered with the lid.

SALAD Squeeze the juice of ½ a lemon into a large serving bowl and add a couple of lugs of extra virgin olive oil and a good pinch of salt & pepper. Finely chop the mint leaves and ½ a chile and add to the bowl. Peel thin slices from as many of the baby zucchini as you can over the dressing and put whatever is left behind on a large wooden cutting board. Take the bowl of salad to the table but don't toss until right before you are ready to serve.

RICE Roughly chop and mix the roasted red peppers and basil leaves on the cutting board with the remaining zucchini. Add a pinch of salt & pepper, a good lug of extra virgin olive oil and a splash of balsamic.

SPRITZER Blitz the berries to a purée in the food processor. Half-fill a large pitcher with ice cubes and rip in the leaves from a few sprigs of mint. Put a strainer on top of the pitcher and quickly push the blitzed berries through, using the back of a spoon. Discard whatever is left behind, then top the pitcher up with sparkling water, stir, and take to the table. Quickly rinse out the processor.

SALMON When the 14 minutes are up, take the pan out of the oven. Using a knife and your fingers, carefully peel the skin away from the flesh and flip it over. Add a pinch of salt and the fennel seeds. Turn the bell peppers over, then put the pan back under the boiler and cook for a further 5 minutes, or until the skin is really crispy.

GUACAMOLE Trim the scallions and put them into the processor with most of the cilantro, the chile (stalk removed), a peeled clove of garlic, the juice of 1 of your limes, and a good drizzle of extra virgin olive oil. Whiz up while you pit the avocados and quarter the tomatoes. Stop whizzing, and squeeze the avocado flesh out of its skin into the processor. Add the tomatoes and pulse until chunky. Put into a bowl and add more seasoning or lime juice to taste if needed. Take to the table with a few wedges of lime for squeezing over.

RICE Quickly fluff up the rice with a fork, then tip over the board of chopped vegetables and gently mix together. Take to the table. Put a grill pan on a high heat.

SALMON Use tongs to carefully turn the crispy salmon skin back over. Season with salt & pepper and cook for a further 5 minutes.

EXTRAS Warm the tortillas one at a time in the grill pan for a few seconds on each side (or stack them up and put them into the microwave for 10 to 15 seconds). Tip the sour cream into a bowl, drizzle over a little extra virgin olive oil, and take to the table.

TO SERVE Take the salmon straight to the table and serve with the lovely salad.

ROAST BEEF
BABY POPOVERS
LITTLE CARROTS
CRISPY POTATOES
SUPER-QUICK GRAVY

SERVES 4

POTATOES

1 pound red-skinned potatoes
1 lemon
4 sprigs of fresh thyme or rosemary
1 head of garlic

BEEF

8 sprigs each of fresh rosemary, sage, and thyme
1½ pounds beef tenderloin

CARROTS

1 pound small carrots
2 sprigs of fresh thyme
2 fresh bay leaves
1 heaping tablespoon sugar
a pat of butter

POPOVERS

scant 1 cup all-purpose flour
1 cup of milk
1 egg

WATERCRESS SALAD

½ red onion
2 tablespoons red wine vinegar
1 tablespoon superfine sugar
1 x 5-ounce package prewashed watercress

GRAVY

½ red onion
12 baby button mushrooms
1 heaping tablespoon all-purpose flour
1 small wineglass of red wine
1¼ cups organic chicken broth

SEASONINGS

olive oil
extra virgin olive oil
sea salt & black pepper

TO SERVE

creamed horseradish sauce
English mustard
a bottle of red wine

TO START Get all your ingredients and equipment ready. Fill and boil the kettle. Turn the oven on to 425°F, and put a 12-cup muffin pan on the top shelf. Put 1 large saucepan and 2 large frying pans on a medium heat. Put the thin slicer disc attachment into the food processor.

POTATOES Wash the potatoes, leaving the skins on. Chop into 1-inch chunks and throw into one of the large frying pans. Cover with boiling water, season with salt, and cover with a lid. Turn the heat right up, and boil for 8 minutes, or until just cooked. Fill and reboil the kettle.

BEEF Quickly pick and finely chop the rosemary, sage, and thyme leaves. Turn the heat under the empty frying pan up to high. Mix the herbs together and spread them around the cutting board with a good pinch of salt & pepper. Cut the fillet in half lengthways, then roll each piece back and forth so they are completely coated in herbs. Add the meat to the hot empty frying pan with a few good lugs of olive oil. You must turn it every minute while you get on with other jobs. Don't forget to touch the ends to the pan to seal in the juices.

CARROTS Tip the carrots into the saucepan and just cover with boiling water. Add 2 sprigs of thyme, a couple of bay leaves, a good pinch of salt, a splash of olive oil, and 1 heaping tablespoon of sugar. Cook with a lid on until tender.

POPOVERS Put the flour, milk, and egg into the blender with a pinch of salt. Blitz, then quickly and confidently remove the muffin pan from the oven and close the door. In one quick movement, back and forth, drizzle a little olive oil in each compartment, then do the same with the batter until each one is ½ to ⅓ full (any remaining batter can be used for crêpes another day). Put in the top of the oven, close the door, and do not open for about 14 minutes, until golden and risen.

POTATOES Check that the potatoes are cooked through, then drain and return to the same frying pan. Leave on a high heat and drizzle over some olive oil. Add a pinch of salt & pepper, peel in thin strips of lemon zest, and add 4 sprigs of thyme or rosemary. Halve the head of garlic widthways, squash each half with the back of a knife, and add to the pan. Toss everything together, then roughly squash down with a masher. Toss every 3 minutes or so, until golden and crisp.

GRAVY Reduce the heat under the beef a little. Peel the red onion half. Thinly slice in the food processor. Add half the onion to the beef pan with a splash of olive oil, the other half to a salad bowl. Rinse the mushrooms in a colander and slice in the processor, then add to the beef pan. Stir everything around and remember to keep turning the beef regularly for 5 minutes.

WATERCRESS SALAD Add 2 tablespoons of red wine vinegar, 1 tablespoon of superfine sugar, and a good pinch of salt & pepper to the onion bowl. Scrunch with one hand. Add ¼ cup extra virgin olive oil. Empty the watercress on top and take to the table, but don't mix until serving.

GRAVY Remove the beef to a plate. Drizzle with a little olive oil, then cover with foil. Stir 1 heaping tablespoon of flour into the pan. Add a small glass of red wine and turn the heat up. Boil down to nearly nothing, then stir in 1¼ cups of chicken broth and simmer until thick and shiny.

TO SERVE Drain the carrots, return to the pan, toss with butter, and take to the table. Turn the potatoes out onto a platter. Smear 2 spoonfuls of horseradish sauce and 1 teaspoon of English mustard onto another platter. Quickly slice the beef ½-inch thick, using long carving motions. Sprinkle over a pinch of salt & pepper from a height, then pile the beef on top of the horseradish sauce and mustard. Add any resting juices to the gravy and serve in a pitcher. Toss and dress the salad quickly, then get the popovers out of the oven, and take them to the table and tuck in with a glass of wine.

STEAK SARNIE

CRISPY BABY POTATOES

CHEESY MUSHROOMS

BEET SALAD

SERVES 4

POTATOES
1 pound baby white potatoes
6 cloves garlic
a few sprigs fresh rosemary
½ lemon

MUSHROOMS
4 large flat Portobello mushrooms
   (approx. 8 ounces in total)
2 cloves garlic
½ fresh red chile
2 sprigs of fresh Italian parsley
½ lemon
3 ounces sharp Cheddar cheese

BEET SALAD
1 x 8-ounce package cooked
   vacuum-packed beets
balsamic vinegar
½ lemon
a bunch of fresh Italian parsley
2 ounces feta cheese

STEAK SARNIE
1½ pounds best-quality sirloin steak
   (cut ½-inch thick)
2 sprigs of fresh thyme
1 ciabatta loaf
a small handful of roasted red
   peppers (from a jar)

a couple of sprigs of fresh Italian
   parsley
horseradish sauce, to serve
a large handful of prewashed arugula,
   to serve

SEASONINGS
olive oil
extra virgin olive oil
sea salt & black pepper

TO START Get all your ingredients and equipment ready. Put a grill pan on medium heat and a large frying pan on high heat. Turn the broiler to full blast. Fill and boil the kettle. Put the coarse grater attachment into the food processor.

POTATOES Cut any large potatoes in half, then add all of them to the large empty frying pan with a good pinch of salt. Quickly squash 6 unpeeled cloves of garlic with the heel of your hand, then add to the pan. Pour in enough boiling water to cover, then cook for 12 to 15 minutes, or until cooked through.

MUSHROOMS Lay the mushrooms, stalk side up, on a cutting board. Trim the stalks and put the mushrooms stalk side up in a small earthenware dish that they fit into fairly snugly. Crush ½ unpeeled clove of garlic over each mushroom. Finely chop ½ chile and a couple of parsley sprigs, and divide between the mushrooms. Grate over the zest of ½ lemon, drizzle well with olive oil, and season. Cut the Cheddar into 4 chunks and put 1 on each mushroom.

BEET SALAD Grate the beets in the food processor. Remove the bowl from the processor, take out the grater attachment, and pour in a couple of lugs of balsamic vinegar and a few lugs of extra virgin olive oil. Squeeze in the juice of ½ lemon. Finely chop a bunch of parsley and add most of it. Stir to dress, then tip into a nice serving bowl. Scatter over the rest of the parsley. Crumble over the feta. Drizzle with extra virgin olive oil and take to the table.

MUSHROOMS Broil on the top shelf for 9 to 10 minutes, or until golden.

STEAK SARNIE Put the steaks on a board. Sprinkle with salt & pepper, pick and scatter over the thyme leaves, and drizzle with olive oil. Rub the flavors into the meat, then flip over and repeat on the other side. Pound the steaks once

or twice with your fists to flatten them a little, then put into the screaming-hot grill pan to cook for 1 to 2 minutes on each side for medium rare, or longer if you prefer. This depends on the thickness of your steaks, of course, so use your instincts and cook them to your liking. Wash your hands.

POTATOES Check they are cooked through, and drain in a colander. Return the pan to a high heat, add a good lug of olive oil, and tip the potatoes and garlic back in. Use a potato masher to lightly burst the skins open (don't mash them though). Add a few sprigs of rosemary and a pinch of salt. Toss every couple of minutes until golden and crisp.

STEAK SARNIE Put the ciabatta loaf into the bottom of the oven. Finely chop the roasted red peppers on a large clean board. Move the steaks to the board and drizzle with extra virgin olive oil. Finely chop a few parsley leaves, mixing them in with the peppers and all the steak juices. Scrape the pepper mix to one side of the board. Slice up the steaks at an angle.

MUSHROOMS Remove the mushrooms from the oven and turn the broiler off. Take the mushrooms straight to the table.

STEAK SARNIE Get the ciabatta out of the oven and slice it open with a serrated knife. Drizzle with extra virgin olive oil from a height. Spread over as much horseradish as you like, then arrange the arugula leaves on one half. Lay the steak slices on top. Mix and scrape the peppers and juices from the board and scatter over the meat, then fold together and take to the table.

POTATOES Tip the potatoes onto a serving platter, and put ½ lemon on the side for squeezing over. Take to the table.

RIB-EYE STIR-FRY

DAN DAN NOODLES

CHILLED HIBISCUS TEA

SERVES 4

STEAKS

1 pound best-quality rib-eye steak
  (cut ½-inch thick)
1 heaping teaspoon Szechuan pepper
Chinese five-spice powder
1-inch piece of fresh gingerroot
½ red chile
1 clove garlic
1 lime
a few sprigs of fresh cilantro

GREENS

6 ounces sugar snap peas
2 baby bok choy
8 ounces broccolini
1 generous tablespoon black bean
  sauce
1 lemon or lime

DAN DAN NOODLES

⅓ cup chili oil
¼ cup soy sauce
1 clove garlic
2½ cups bean sprouts
½ bunch fresh cilantro
8 scallions
14 ounces dried medium Chinese egg
  noodles (chow mein noodles)
1 organic beef bouillon cube
½ lemon
honey
a squeeze of lime juice

SEASONINGS

olive oil
extra virgin olive oil
sea salt & black pepper

HIBISCUS TEA

2–3 hibiscus, mint, or jasmine
  tea bags
1 clementine
1 lime
1 heaping soup spoon sugar
a few handfuls of ice
a few sprigs of fresh mint

TO START Get all your ingredients and equipment ready. Fill and boil the kettle. Put a grill pan on high heat and a large saucepan on low heat. Get out 4 serving bowls.

STEAKS Put the meat on a wooden board and sprinkle salt & pepper from a height over the meat and board. Pound the Szechuan pepper using a pestle & mortar. Put a tiny pinch in each serving bowl, then sprinkle the rest over the meat along with a really good pinch of five-spice. Drizzle a little olive oil over the meat and board, then rub the meat all over the board so it picks up the flavors really well.

DAN DAN NOODLES Pour boiling water into the large saucepan. Turn the heat up to high and cover with a lid. Fill and reboil the kettle. Pour 1½ to 2 tablespoons of chili oil and 1 tablespoon of soy sauce into each serving bowl. Crush 1 unpeeled clove of garlic and divide the pulped flesh between the bowls.

HIBISCUS TEA Put the tea bags into a large pitcher, then use a peeler to peel off the zest of the clementine and the lime into long strips. Add the zest to the pitcher along with the sugar. Fill the pitcher halfway with boiling water and leave to steep.

STEAKS Put the steak on the hot grill pan to cook for 2 minutes on each side for medium rare, or until cooked to your liking. Use tongs to turn them while you get on with other jobs.

DAN DAN NOODLES Get the garnishes ready. Put the bean sprouts in a serving bowl with the cilantro and take to the table.

GREENS Season the boiling water with a pinch of salt and add the sugar snap peas. Flip over the board you dressed the meat on, then halve the bok choy. Trim the ends off the broccolini lengthways, then add to the pan with the bok choy and sugar snap peas. Put the lid on.

DAN DAN NOODLES Trim and thinly slice the scallions and divide them between the serving bowls. (Don't forget to check the steaks – they should be perfect now.)

STEAKS Get a clean board, drizzle it with olive oil, and lay your steaks on top. Take the grill pan off the heat. Peel the ginger, then finely grate it, with the chile and garlic, over the steaks, just to flavor and perfume. Squeeze over the lime juice.

GREENS Spoon 1 generous tablespoon of black bean sauce into the middle of a platter and spread around. Squeeze over the lemon or lime juice and drizzle over a lug of olive oil. Use tongs and a slotted spoon to fish out all the peas and greens, holding them up for a minute to let some of the excess water drip away, then pile on top of the black bean sauce. Drizzle over a little extra virgin olive oil and take to the table to toss and dress at the last minute.

HIBISCUS TEA Remove the tea bags. Add a few large handfuls of ice to the hibiscus tea, then halve the clementine and the lime and squeeze in all their juices. Add both halves of lime and the sprigs of mint to the pitcher.

DAN DAN NOODLES Add the noodles to the water you used for the greens, with 1 bouillon cube. Squeeze a few drips of lemon juice and ½ teaspoon of honey into each serving bowl.

STEAKS Slice the steaks at an angle into ½-inch strips, then toss so they mop up all the flavorful juices on the board. Tear over the cilantro and take to the table.

DAN DAN NOODLES Use tongs to divide the noodles between the bowls. Ladle over a little broth and take to the table. Get everyone to toss their noodles, then assemble their own bowl by dressing it with garnishes and adding a pinch of bean sprouts, some cilantro leaves, some greens, a few strips of steak and a squeeze or two of lime juice.

SUPER-FAST BEEF HASH

BAKED POTATOES

GODDESS SALAD

LOVELY BUTTER BEANS & BACON

SERVES 4

POTATOES
4 large baking potatoes
2 sprigs of fresh rosemary
4 teaspoons sour cream

HASH
1 pound good-quality ground beef
2 sprigs of fresh thyme
1 red onion
2 carrots
3 celery stalks
a few sprigs of fresh rosemary

4 cloves garlic
⅓ cup Worcestershire sauce (such as
  Lea & Perrins)
a small bunch of fresh Italian parsley

BEANS
4 slices of smoked bacon
2 tomatoes
1 x 15-ounce can butter beans
  or cannellini beans
red wine vinegar
2 or 3 sprigs of fresh Greek basil or
  basil, leaves picked

SALAD
1 bibb lettuce
a handful of prewashed watercress
1 avocado
1 generous tablespoon sour cream
1 lemon

SEASONINGS
olive oil
extra virgin olive oil
sea salt & black pepper

TO START Get all your ingredients and equipment ready. Turn the broiler on to full blast and put a baking sheet underneath it to heat up. Put a large frying pan on medium-high heat and another on low heat. Put the thin slicer disc attachment into the food processor.

POTATOES Wash the potatoes, trim off any gnarly bits, stab a few times with a knife, then put into a large microwave-safe bowl and cover with a double layer of plastic wrap. Put straight into the microwave for around 14 to 16 minutes, or until cooked.

HASH Put the beef into the largest frying pan and break it up with a wooden spoon. Add 1 teaspoon of salt and 1 teaspoon of pepper, and drizzle over some olive oil. Pick in the thyme leaves and cook until golden, stirring often.

BEANS Drizzle olive oil into the second frying pan on a low heat. Thinly slice the bacon and add to the pan. Toss occasionally and move the pan off the heat once the bacon is golden.

HASH Peel and halve the red onion. Wash and trim the carrots and celery, then slice all of them in the food processor and set aside. When the beef is golden, pick the rosemary leaves into the pan. Crush in the 4 unpeeled cloves of garlic and add ⅓ cup of Worcestershire sauce. Stir well, cook until nicely glazed, then add the sliced veggies and stir again. Reduce the heat to medium and remember to toss often.

POTATOES Put a knife through each potato to check they are cooked through. Pick and finely chop the rosemary leaves, and add them to the bowl with a pinch of salt & pepper and a drizzle of olive oil. Gently toss to coat them in the flavors, then use tongs to transfer the potatoes to the hot baking sheet and put under the broiler to crisp up.

BEANS Now get your pan of bacon on high heat. Roughly chop the tomatoes and add them to the bacon. Tip in the beans and their juices, and simmer gently to cook the liquid down.

SALAD Pull the leaves off the lettuce, then wash and spin them dry. Put into a serving bowl with the watercress. Halve and pit the avocado, then use a spoon to scoop slivers from one half into the serving bowl. Whiz the sour cream in a blender with the remaining avocado flesh, the juice of 1 lemon, ¼ cup extra virgin olive oil, and a pinch of salt & pepper. If it's too thick, add a splash or two of water until you have a creamy dressing.

HASH Finely chop the parsley. Add most of it to the hash pan, reserving a few leaves. Taste and correct the seasoning, then transfer it to a large serving platter.

POTATOES Take the potatoes out of the oven. Cut a cross on each one and pinch them open. Serve on top of the hash. Top each with 1 teaspoon of sour cream and scatter over the remaining parsley. Take the platter to the table.

BEANS Add a little extra virgin olive oil and a good splash of vinegar, then season. Sprinkle over the Greek basil leaves. Take the pan to the table.

SALAD Toss with the dressing and tuck in!

STEAK
INDIAN-STYLE

SPINACH & PANEER SALAD

NAAN BREADS

MANGO DESSERT

SERVES 4

STEAKS

¼ x 10-ounce jar Patak's jalfrezi
  (medium) curry paste*
½ lemon
2 pounds best-quality sirloin steak
  (cut ½-inch thick)
a few sprigs of fresh cilantro

YOGURT DIP

1 cup plain yogurt
a few sprigs of fresh mint
½ lemon

NAAN BREADS

2 naan breads, or other flatbreads

PANEER & SPINACH SALAD

2 x 5-ounce packages prewashed baby
  spinach
a small bunch of fresh cilantro
1 cup alfalfa sprouts
1 cup sprouted cress, or extra alfalfa
1 large carrot
8 ounces paneer cheese
3 tablespoons sesame seeds
1 lemon

CURRY SAUCE

¼ x 10-ounce jar Patak's jalfrezi
  (medium) curry paste*
½ x 14-ounce can coconut milk

SEASONINGS

olive oil
extra virgin olive oil
sea salt & black pepper

MANGO DESSERT

2 ripe mangoes
1 heaping teaspoon confectioners'
  sugar
a few sprigs of fresh mint
1 lime

TO START Get all your ingredients and equipment ready. Put a grill pan on high heat. Turn the oven on to 375°F.

STEAKS Dollop ¼ of the jar of jalfrezi paste into a large flat bowl and mix in the juice of ½ lemon, a few good lugs of olive oil, and a good pinch of salt & pepper. Put the steaks on top, rub this marinade all over them, then set aside and wash your hands.

YOGURT DIP Spoon the yogurt into a dish. Thinly slice the leafy tops of the sprigs of mint, then add to the yogurt with a drizzle of extra virgin olive oil, the juice of ½ lemon, and a good pinch of salt. Take to the table and stir just before serving.

PANEER & SPINACH SALAD Tip the spinach onto a platter. Tear and scatter over most of the cilantro leaves. Scatter over the alfalfa sprouts and cress. Use a peeler to peel the carrot into ribbons on top.

NAAN BREADS Scrunch up a large piece of parchment paper under the tap, then flatten out and drizzle with olive oil. Wrap the naans in the paper and put into the oven to warm through.

STEAKS Use tongs to transfer the steaks to the screaming-hot grill pan. Cook for about 6 minutes in total, turning every minute, for medium-rare steaks, around 8 minutes in total for medium, and about 10 minutes for well done. You know how you like your meat, so use your instincts and move it to a board once cooked to your liking. Put a small frying pan on medium heat.

CURRY SAUCE Put a small saucepan on medium heat. Add ¼ of the jar of jalfrezi paste, pour in ½ the can of coconut milk, mix well, then leave to bubble and thicken.

*Patak's curry paste is available online.

PANEER & SPINACH SALAD Chop the paneer into bite-sized pieces and add to the hot frying pan with a splash of olive oil. Check on your steaks.

CURRY SAUCE Once the sauce has boiled down to a nice consistency, turn the heat underneath down to low, or turn off. Check your steaks again.

PANEER & SPINACH SALAD Turn the paneer over – it should be nicely golden underneath. Add a good pinch of salt and 3 tablespoons of sesame seeds. Turn the heat down if it looks like it's cooking too fast.

MANGO DESSERT Slice both mangoes down either side of the pit. Take each half and score a crisscross pattern about ¾ inch down through the flesh, stopping at the skin. Turn the skin inside out so the mango pieces pop up. Trim the skin off the middle bit where the pit is, then either chop chunks of flesh off or eat them as a treat (🍽)!

Arrange the mango porcupines on a board and dust 1 heaping teaspoon of confectioners' sugar all over, then finely chop a few mint leaves and sprinkle over. Slice the lime into wedges for serving. Take to the table.

STEAKS If you haven't already done so, move the steaks to a board to rest and drizzle over a little extra virgin olive oil.

PANEER & SPINACH SALAD Arrange the paneer around the edge of the salad and cut the lemon into wedges for squeezing over. Take to the table.

TO SERVE Slice up the meat at an angle, toss in the resting juices and oil from the board, and scatter over the cilantro leaves. Tip the warm curry sauce into a bowl and take to the table with the stack of warm naan breads and the sliced steak.

MEATBALL SANDWICH

PICKLED CABBAGE

CHOPPED SALAD

BANANA ICE CREAM

SERVES 4–6

MEATBALL SANDWICH

a small handful of fresh basil
1 pound good-quality ground beef
1 tablespoon whole-grain mustard
½ lemon
1 egg
8 slices smoked pancetta
2 ciabatta loaves
4 slices Jarlsberg cheese

CABBAGE

½ small red cabbage
1 red onion
a small bunch of fresh mint
1 fresh red chile
2 lemons

CHOPPED SALAD

½ English (hothouse) cucumber
2 tomatoes
2 avocados
a handful of fresh basil leaves
1 x 5-ounce package prewashed
  Italian salad mix
1 teaspoon English mustard
1½ tablespoons red wine vinegar
2 ounces feta cheese

SEASONINGS

olive oil
extra virgin olive oil
sea salt & black pepper

ICE CREAM

6 bananas (approx. 2 pounds), peeled,
  sliced and put into the freezer in
  sandwich bags at least 6 hours in
  advance
1 cup low-fat plain yogurt
1 tablespoon honey
2–3 handfuls of unsweetened
  shredded coconut for coating
8 sweet, crunchy cookies

TO SERVE

cold beer

NOTE: Make sure your bananas are frozen ahead of time, at least 6 hours before. Peel and slice them, then put in sandwich bags in the freezer. This is a great habit to get into, especially with fruit that is starting to become overripe.

TO START Get all your ingredients and equipment ready. Turn the oven on to 320°F. Take the bananas out of the freezer. Put a large ovenproof frying pan on a medium heat. Put the thin slicer disc attachment into the food processor. Get 4 old-fashioned glasses out for dessert, then check your freezer to make sure you have room for them.

MEATBALL SANDWICH Roughly chop the basil and put it into a large mixing bowl with the ground beef, whole-grain mustard, a pinch of salt & pepper, and the zest of ½ lemon. Separate the egg and add the yolk to the bowl with 1 tablespoon of olive oil. Add a drizzle of olive oil to the ovenproof frying pan, then really scrunch and mix up the beef mixture with clean hands. Quickly divide the beef mixture into 4, then divide each portion into 4 again. Work quickly to pat, roll, and shape these into meatballs (it helps if you wet your hands as you do this). Put them in the pan as you go, then wash your hands. Shake, toss, and cook the meatballs for about 12 to 14 minutes, or until they are golden all over.

CABBAGE Slice off the base of the cabbage half, peel off the outer leaves, and cut into 4 wedges. Push them into the food processor to thinly slice. Peel and halve the onion, rip the top half off the bunch of mint, and add to the processor with the chile (stalk removed).

MEATBALL SANDWICH Uncoil and lay the pancetta slices in the frying pan, around the meatballs, and put into the oven with the ciabattas on the shelf underneath.

CABBAGE Tip the shredded veggies and chile into a large bowl and add a good lug of extra virgin olive oil. Squeeze over the lemon juice and add a good pinch of salt. Toss everything together.

CHOPPED SALAD I like to use 2 knives for this, but do whatever feels safe and comfortable. Roughly chop the cucumber and tomatoes together on a really large board. Halve and pit the avocados. Spoon out the avocado flesh, add it to the cucumber and tomatoes, and chop again. Add the basil leaves and continue chopping. Tip the salad leaves onto the board on top of the rest of the salad. Make a well in the center of the leaves, then add a teaspoon of English mustard, a pinch of salt, 5 tablespoons of extra virgin olive oil, and 1½ tablespoons of red wine vinegar. Chop and toss again to dress. Add more olive oil if needed, then crumble over the feta.

ICE CREAM Quickly wash the food processor bowl with cold water, then swap in the standard blade attachment and whiz the frozen bananas with yogurt and honey until thick and creamy. Put the shredded coconut into a large bowl, then take 1 soup spoon of banana ice cream and roll it in coconut until covered. Do this with each scoop, putting them into glasses as you go. Once you've used up all the ice cream, put the glasses into the freezer until you're ready for dessert.

MEATBALL SANDWICH Remove the pan of meatballs and ciabattas from the oven. Open out the hot ciabattas, drizzle over a little extra virgin olive oil, lay 2 slices of Jarlsberg on each loaf, scatter over some cabbage salad, then top with meatballs and a few slices of crispy pancetta.

TO SERVE Take the meatball sandwiches to the table with the chopped salad. Squeeze the sandwiches shut, halve them, then dive in. When ready, get the banana ice cream out of the freezer and enjoy with a crunchy cookie.

LIVER & BACON

ONION GRAVY

SMASHED POTATOES

DRESSED GREENS

BERRY & CUSTARD RIPPLE

SERVES 4

POTATOES
1 pound red-skinned potatoes
1 lemon

GRAVY
2 red onions
a few sprigs of fresh rosemary
1 teaspoon honey
2 cloves garlic
1 heaping tablespoon all-purpose flour
1 wineglass of red wine
3 tablespoons balsamic vinegar
1 organic beef bouillon cube

LIVER
8 slices of smoked bacon
12 ounces calves' liver
all-purpose flour
4 sprigs of fresh rosemary

GREENS
8 ounces of Swiss chard or other
  seasonal greens
½ lemon

SEASONINGS
olive oil
extra virgin olive oil
sea salt & black pepper

BERRY DESSERT
1 x 15-ounce can peaches or
  pears in juice
1 heaping cup blueberries,
  blackberries, or other nice berries
3 or 4 tablespoons elderflower
  cordial, optional*
1¾ cups good-quality custard or 1
  cup heavy cream, lightly whipped*
¾ cup Greek yogurt
1 teaspoon vanilla paste or extract
a few Scottish shortbread cookies,
  to serve

TO START Get all your ingredients and equipment ready. Fill and boil the kettle. Put a 3-level steamer pan and 2 large frying pans on a medium heat. Put the thin slicer disc attachment into the food processor.

POTATOES Wash the potatoes. Leave the skins on but remove any gnarly bits. Cut into generous 1-inch pieces. Fill the steamer pan with boiled water, add a pinch of salt and the potatoes and put the lid on.

BERRY DESSERT Pour the juice from the canned fruit into a large saucepan on a high heat and bring to a boil.

GRAVY Peel and halve the red onions and slice up in the food processor. Put into one of the hot frying pans with a splash of olive oil and stir. Pick and finely chop the rosemary leaves and add them to the pan with the teaspoon of honey. Crush in 2 peeled cloves of garlic. Stir occasionally while you get on with the rest of the meal.

LIVER Put the bacon into the other frying pan with a lug of olive oil. Keep turning it until golden on both sides, then move to a plate and take the pan off the heat.

BERRY DESSERT Add the canned fruit and fresh berries to the pan and stir occasionally until thick.

GREENS Wash the chard well. Thinly slice the stalks and add to the lowest pan of the steamer. Roughly chop the larger leaves and add to the top level of the steamer. Stack both above the potatoes and put the lid on. Refill and boil the kettle.

GRAVY Stir the heaping tablespoon of flour into the pan of onions. Add the glass of red wine. Cook away, then add the 3 tablespoons of balsamic vinegar and stir again. Add the beef bouillon cube and 1¼ cups of boiled water. Stir and simmer until it's a good consistency.

BERRY DESSERT This should be lovely and jam-like by now, so turn the heat off and stir in 3 or 4 tablespoons of elderflower cordial to taste, if using. Spoon the custard or cream around a serving bowl, then pour the fruit and syrup into the center. Dollop over the yogurt, spoon over 1 teaspoon of vanilla paste or extract, then fold and ripple through. Take to the table with a few shortbread cookies.

LIVER Put the bacon pan back on the heat. Lay the liver on parchment paper. Season with salt & pepper and dust both sides with an even coating of flour. Turn the heat up under the pan and add the liver and a splash more olive oil. Don't be tempted to turn it. Leave to cook for 3 minutes.

POTATOES Check the potatoes are cooked through, then drain them and mash with a really good drizzle of extra virgin olive oil, a good pinch of salt & pepper, and a few gratings of lemon zest. Spoon onto a large serving platter.

LIVER Turn the liver over, add the rosemary sprigs, and return the bacon to the pan. Cook for 2 more minutes, then lay it on top of the potatoes and take the platter to the table.

GREENS Put the chard on a serving dish, drizzle over some extra virgin olive oil, and squeeze over the juice of ½ lemon. Add a pinch of salt & pepper and take to the table.

TO SERVE Pour the gravy into a pitcher and you're ready to tuck in.

*Elderflower cordial and canned custard are available online.

STUFFED FOCACCIA

PROSCIUTTO

CELERY ROOT REMOULADE

DRESSED MOZZARELLA

FRESH LEMON & LIME GRANITA

SERVES 4–6

FOCACCIA

1 x 16-ounce focaccia loaf
1 x 16-ounce jar roasted red peppers
1 teaspoon capers, drained
6 sun-dried tomatoes in oil
a large handful of good-quality mixed marinated olives
1 fresh red chile
a large handful of cherry or grape tomatoes
3 or 4 cornichons
a small bunch of fresh mint
½ lemon
Parmesan cheese, for grating

REMOULADE & PROSCIUTTO

1 celery root (approx. 1½ pounds)
½ fresh red chile
1 pear
a bunch of fresh Italian parsley
1 teaspoon Dijon mustard
1 teaspoon whole-grain mustard
2 tablespoons white wine vinegar
8 ounces good-quality prosciutto

PESTO & MOZZARELLA

8 ounces fresh mozzarella
¾ cup pinenuts
½ clove of garlic
3 ounces Parmesan cheese
a large bunch of fresh basil
optional: a few sprigs of fresh basil
½ lemon
½ dried chile

SEASONINGS

extra virgin olive oil
sea salt & black pepper

GRANITA

1 bag of ice cubes
3 or 4 sprigs of fresh mint
1 lemon
1 lime
1 teaspoon vanilla paste or extract
3 heaping tablespoons superfine sugar
1 pink grapefruit
plain yogurt, to serve
1 cup raspberries, to serve

TO SERVE

1 bottle of chilled rosé wine

TO START Get all your ingredients and equipment ready. Turn the oven on to 300°F and put the standard blade attachment into the food processor. Check you have room in your freezer for a platter.

GRANITA Half-fill the food processor with ice cubes. Add the leaves from 3 or 4 sprigs of mint. Finely grate in the zest of the lemon and the lime and add a teaspoon of vanilla paste or extract, then leave to blitz to a sort of snow. While blitzing, add 3 heaping tablespoons of superfine sugar and squeeze in the juice of the lemon and lime. Once the mixture is like snow, spread it over a serving platter and put it straight into the freezer.

REMOULADE & PROSCIUTTO Quickly rinse the food processor, then swap the standard blade for the coarse grater attachment. Halve and peel the celery root, then cut it into wedges. Seed ½ chile, trim the stalk and base of the pear, and halve it lengthways. Grate the celery root, ½ chile, the pear, and a bunch of parsley in the processor. Tip everything into a large bowl. Add a teaspoon each of Dijon and whole-grain mustard, 5 tablespoons of extra virgin olive oil, 2 tablespoons of white wine vinegar, and a pinch of salt & pepper. Toss together gently with your hands, have a taste to check the flavors, and set aside.

FOCACCIA Put the focaccia into the oven to warm for around 15 minutes. Make your pickle filling: put the roasted red peppers, 1 teaspoon of capers, 6 sun-dried tomatoes, a handful of mixed olives, the chile, a handful of cherry tomatoes, and 3 or 4 cornichons on a chopping board. Pick the leaves from the mint. Remove the pits from the olives. Thinly slice the chile, then chop and slice all the filling ingredients together on the board and sweep into a bowl. Add a lug of extra virgin olive oil, squeeze over the juice of ½ lemon, then scrunch and mix together with your hands.

Take the focaccia out of the oven. Carefully halve it across the middle with a sharp serrated bread knife and open it like a book. Spread the pickle filling over the bottom half, drizzle over any juices left behind in the bowl, and finely grate over a good layer of Parmesan. Put the top on the sandwich and take it to the table.

REMOULADE & PROSCIUTTO Arrange the prosciutto around a rustic serving board, then place your celery root remoulade in the center and take to the table.

PESTO & MOZZARELLA Drain the mozzarella and put into a bowl. Give the food processor a quick rinse, then swap the grater attachment for the standard blade. Whiz up ¾ cup of pinenuts, 3 ounces of Parmesan, ½ peeled clove of garlic, and a large bunch of basil with 7 tablespoons of extra virgin olive oil. Spoon 2 tablespoons of this pesto over the mozzarella, then put the rest in a screw-top jar for another day. Drizzle over some extra virgin olive oil and a pinch of salt & pepper. Toss and dress the mozzarella in the flavors, then sprinkle over the leaves from a few sprigs of Greek basil, if using, and drizzle over some more extra virgin olive oil. Squeeze over the juice of ½ lemon, quickly grate over some Parmesan, crumble over the dried chile half, then move the mozzarella to a serving dish and take to the table.

TO SERVE Divide the focaccia sandwich and dressed mozzarella up between everyone. Serve with a few slices of prosciutto, some of the crunchy remoulade, and a glass of chilled rosé.

GRANITA When you're ready for dessert, take the platter of granita out of the freezer. Use a fork to fluff up the ice and squeeze over the juice of the pink grapefruit. Take to the table with the plain yogurt and raspberries. Delicious!

SEARED PORK FILLET & CATHERINE WHEEL SAUSAGE

MEATY MUSHROOM SAUCE

CELERY ROOT SMASH

GARLICKY BEANS

SERVES 6

PORK

1 pound good-quality pork tenderloin
1 pound good-quality skinny
  breakfast sausage links
4 sprigs of fresh rosemary
2 small red apples
sugar

CELERY ROOT

1 celery root (approx. 2 pounds)
a few sprigs of fresh thyme
½ lemon

SAUCE

4 slices smoked bacon
a few sprigs of fresh rosemary
8 ounces pork kidney
8 medium white or crimini
  mushrooms
optional: a slug of Marsala
⅔ cup heavy cream
1 tablespoon English mustard

BEANS

1 pound green beans
½ lemon
1 clove garlic

SEASONINGS

olive oil
extra virgin olive oil
sea salt & black pepper

TO SERVE

good brown ale

TO START Get all your ingredients and equipment ready. Turn the oven on to 425°F. Put your largest ovenproof frying pan on a high heat and a medium frying pan on medium heat. Fill and boil the kettle.

PORK Butterfly the pork tenderloin by halving it lengthways but leaving it joined at the top so it opens out like a book (or ask your butcher to do this for you). Drizzle with olive oil, scatter over a good pinch of salt & pepper, then rub all over so it's well coated. Wash your hands. Put into the large ovenproof frying pan and keep turning it every minute or so for around 5 minutes, while you do other jobs, until golden on all sides.

CELERY ROOT Get a clean board, then quickly peel the celery root with a knife or a vegetable peeler and chop into large chunks (🔪). Put into a large microwave-safe serving bowl with a good pinch of salt & pepper. Pick the thyme leaves into the bowl. Squeeze in the juice of ½ lemon. Add a tiny splash of boiled water and the lemon half, then cover the bowl with a double layer of plastic wrap. Microwave on full power for around 12 minutes, or until tender. Wash the board and the knife.

PORK Add a splash of olive oil to the tenderloin if needed. Turn the heat down a little and keep turning for another couple of minutes.

SAUCE Slice the bacon thinly and put into the empty frying pan with a drizzle of olive oil. Pick in the leaves from a few sprigs of rosemary. Halve the kidney, removing any white bits of sinew. Thinly slice the mushrooms and kidney and add to the pan with a really good pinch of pepper. Stir well.

PORK Coil the sausages around so you end up with a Catherine wheel (just like in the picture) and secure with skewers (🔪). Use tongs to move the tenderloin to a roasting pan, then put into the oven on the top shelf to cook for 15 minutes, or until golden on both sides. Add a splash of olive oil to the empty frying pan and lay the Catherine wheel in the pan. Brown on both sides, then leave to cook while you

pick some more rosemary leaves into the pan. Turn over the sausage. Halve the apples, then add them to the pan and move them around so they pick up all the juices.

SAUCE Hold the frying pan carefully and add a good slug of Marsala, if using. Let the alcohol boil off for a minute or light it; after 30 seconds pour in ⅔ cup heavy cream and stir in 1 tablespoon of English mustard.

BEANS Put a small saucepan on a high heat, fill it ¾ full with boiled water, and add a pinch of salt. Trim the beans by cutting across all their ends at once. Add the beans to the water, put a lid on, and cook for 5 minutes, or until tender enough to eat.

PORK Sprinkle a little pinch of sugar over each apple, then put the frying pan on the middle shelf of the oven to continue cooking for 10 minutes while you finish everything off.

CELERY ROOT Get the bowl out of the microwave, check the celery root is cooked, and if so discard the lemon half and any excess water. Add a lug of extra virgin olive oil and season with salt & pepper. Mash until it's a nice consistency. Take to the table.

SAUCE Go back to the creamy mushrooms. Stir in a little cooking water from the beans to thin the sauce, if necessary, then taste, adjusting the seasoning if needed and take straight to the table.

BEANS Drain in a colander, then tip onto a platter. Squeeze over the juice of ½ lemon and crush over an unpeeled clove of garlic. Drizzle over some good-quality extra virgin olive oil, add a pinch of salt & pepper, then toss and take to the table.

TO SERVE Put the sausages and the pork on a wooden board and take to the table with the platter of beans. Let the pork rest for a minute or two while everyone helps themselves, then slice up and serve with some good brown ale.

PORK CHOPS & CRISPY CRACKLINS

CRUSHED POTATOES

MINTY CABBAGE

PEACHES 'N' CUSTARD

SERVES 4

PORK
4 x 6-ounce center cut pork loin
  chops, bone in and skin on
8 cloves garlic
1 teaspoon fennel seeds
a small bunch of fresh sage
honey, for drizzling

POTATOES
1½ pounds Yukon Gold potatoes
½ lemon
1 heaping teaspoon whole-grain
  mustard
a small bunch of fresh Italian parsley

CABBAGE
1 small Savoy cabbage
2 generous teaspoons good-quality
  mint sauce

SEASONINGS
olive oil
extra virgin olive oil
sea salt & black pepper

PEACHES 'N' CUSTARD
2 x 15-ounce cans peach halves in juice
1 cinnamon stick
1¾ cups good-quality custard or
  1 cup heavy cream
4 Scottish shortbread cookies
a couple of sprigs of fresh mint

TO START Get all your ingredients and equipment ready. Turn the oven on to 350°F. Fill and boil the kettle and put a large frying pan on a high heat.

PORK Put the pork chops on a plastic cutting board and trim off the skin and some of the fat. Cut the skin into ½-inch slices and put them into the frying pan, fat side down, to make cracklins.

POTATOES Wash the potatoes and get rid of any gnarly bits. Cut any large ones in half, quickly stab any whole ones, and put into a large microwave-safe serving bowl. Add ½ lemon and a good pinch of salt & pepper. Cover with a double layer of plastic wrap and microwave on full power for around 17 minutes, or until cooked through.

PORK Use tongs to flip the cracklins over. Score across the fat on the chops all the way along, then season on both sides with a good pinch of salt & pepper. Take the pan off the heat once the cracklins are crisp and golden.

CABBAGE Halve the cabbage, trim the base, and remove the outer leaves. Cut into 8 wedges, put into a large saucepan, and set aside.

PORK Lightly squash 8 unpeeled cloves of garlic with the heel of your hand and add to the frying pan – put it back on the heat if you've taken it off. Push the cracklins and garlic to the sides of the pan, then stand all 4 chops up in the pan with the fat side down (look at the picture to see what I mean). Use the tongs to transfer the cracklins and garlic to a roasting pan. Scatter the fennel seeds into the roasting pan, then put it into the oven on the top shelf. Wash your hands well, then pick the sage leaves.

CABBAGE Pour boiled water into the saucepan and add a good pinch of salt. Put the lid on and turn the heat underneath to high. Cook the cabbage for 6 to 8 minutes, or until tender enough to eat.

PORK Once the chops are golden on the fat edge, use the tongs to lay them flat in the pan. Cook for around 4 minutes, turning until golden. Get the cracklins pan out of the oven and add the sage leaves and the pork chops. Mix together, then arrange the sage leaves and cracklins over the pork chops. Drizzle the chops with a little honey from a height, then return the pan to the oven for around 10 minutes, or until the chops are cooked through and look amazing.

PEACHES 'N' CUSTARD Pour the peaches and their juices into a small saucepan. Add the cinnamon stick and put over a high heat. Leave for a few minutes.

CABBAGE Drain the cabbage in a colander, then return it to the pan and stir in 2 generous teaspoons of mint sauce, a pinch of salt & pepper, and a splash of extra virgin olive oil. Gently toss with tongs. Pop the lid back on so it stays warm, and take to the table.

POTATOES Get the potatoes out of the microwave. Carefully pierce and remove the plastic wrap. Check they are cooked, then discard the lemon half. Add 1 heaping teaspoon of mustard, a few good lugs of extra virgin olive oil, and a good pinch of salt & pepper. Finely chop the parsley and add. Break and crush the potatoes with a spoon, mixing all the flavors together. Take to the table.

PEACHES 'N' CUSTARD Drizzle the custard over a platter; or lightly whip the cream and spread over a platter. Spoon the hot peaches on top, and crumble over the shortbread. Drizzle over a little of the warm cooking juices, discarding the rest, then pick the leaves from the mint sprigs and tear over the top.

PORK Remove the pork from the oven and take it straight to the table. Serve with the lovely minty cabbage and crushed potatoes.

KINDA SAUSAGE CASSOULET

WARM BROCCOLINI SALAD

MERINGUES

SERVES 4

244

CASSOULET

4 slices smoked bacon
1½ red onions
a few sprigs of fresh rosemary
½ small bunch of fresh sage
3 fresh bay leaves
2 leeks
1 pound good-quality sausages
3–4 thick slices of bread
2 cloves of garlic
2¾ cups passata or tomato sauce
1 x 15-ounce can butter beans or
  cannellini beans
1 x 15-ounce can navy beans

BROCCOLINI

1 pound broccolini
¼ small red onion
1 clove garlic
2 ripe plum tomatoes
1 lemon

SEASONINGS

olive oil
extra virgin olive oil
sea salt & black pepper

DESSERT

1 heaping cup raspberries or
  strawberries
1 tablespoon honey, plus a little
  extra
¼ cup Greek yogurt
4 extra large meringue cookies or
  2 ounces small meringue cookies
4 teaspoons good-quality lemon curd
a few fresh baby mint leaves

TO SERVE

a bottle of red wine

TO START Get all your ingredients and equipment ready. Turn the broiler to full blast. Fill and boil the kettle. Put the standard blade attachment into the food processor.

CASSOULET Cut the bacon into ½-inch pieces and add to a sturdy roasting pan with a few lugs of olive oil. Put over a high heat. Halve, peel and slice 1½ red onions. Pick the rosemary and most of the sage leaves and sprinkle into the pan with the bay leaves, keeping a few sage sprigs back for later. Trim the leeks and peel back the outer leaves. Cut down the length of the leeks, then wash away any grit and thinly slice. Add the leeks and onions to the pan with a few splashes of boiled water, stir, then leave to soften. Lay the sausages in another roasting pan, drizzle and rub a little olive oil over them, then put under the broiler to cook for 8 minutes. Stir your vegetables.

BROCCOLINI Put a small saucepan on high heat. Trim and discard the ends of the broccolini.

DESSERT Put half the berries in a bowl with 1 tablespoon of honey and mash until soft. Add the Greek yogurt and gently swirl and marble through, then put into the refrigerator. Put the meringue cookies on a serving board, with 1 teaspoon of lemon curd in the center of each. Leave them like this until you're ready to serve them, then dollop a spoonful of your berry yogurt mixture over each one. Top with a few berries, a drizzle of honey, and a few small mint leaves. If using small meringue cookies, then crush them slightly and divide between 4 small glasses, and put a teaspoon of lemon curd on top of the meringues. Finish with the yogurt, berries, honey, and mint just before serving.

CASSOULET Tear the slices of bread into large chunks and put into a food processor with a pinch of salt & pepper, ½ of the reserved sprigs of sage, 2 cloves of garlic, and a good drizzle of olive oil. Pulse until you have fairly even, coarse breadcrumbs. Stir the passata or tomato sauce and the beans and their juices into the pan of vegetables.

BROCCOLINI Peel and coarsely grate ¼ red onion into a mixing bowl. Crush over 1 clove of garlic. Halve the 2 plum tomatoes, discard the seeds, then carefully grate them, flesh-side down, through the coarse grater. Discard the skins left behind. Add a couple of lugs of extra virgin olive oil, season carefully, then squeeze in the juice of 1 lemon and mix.

CASSOULET Take the sausages from under the broiler. Sprinkle half the breadcrumbs from the food processor over the veggies and beans. Lay the sausages dark side down and sprinkle over the rest of the breadcrumbs. Pick the rest of the sage leaves, drizzle with olive oil, and scatter on top. Put the roasting pan into the oven under the broiler on the middle shelf for around 4 minutes, or until the breadcrumbs are crisp and golden and the sausages are cooked through.

BROCCOLINI Put the broccolini, stalks down, into a pan of boiling water and put the lid on. Cook for a couple of minutes, or until tender.

TO SERVE The broccolini should be tender by now, so drain it, then scatter on a platter and spoon over the dressing. Toss quickly, and take straight to the table. Remove the cassoulet from the oven and take to the table with a nice bottle of red wine.

BRITISH PICNIC

SERVES 4 (with great leftovers or 8 as a light lunch)

SAUSAGE ROLLS, MACKEREL PÂTÉ, LOVELY ASPARAGUS CRUNCH SALAD, PIMM'S ETON MESS

SAUSAGE ROLLS
all-purpose flour, for dusting
1 large sheet all-butter puff pastry
  (14-ounce package), thawed if frozen
1 egg
12 skinny breakfast sausage links
  (approx. 14 ounces)
1 teaspoon fennel seeds
Parmesan cheese, for grating
1 tablespoon sesame seeds

ASPARAGUS
1 bunch asparagus
½ lemon
Good-quality aged Cheddar cheese,
  to serve

PÂTÉ
1 heaping soup spoon creamed
  horseradish
12 ounces smoked mackerel
1 x 8-ounce bar reduced-fat cream
  cheese (Neufchâtel)
a bunch of fresh Italian parsley
2 lemons
1 small bunch of radishes
a loaf of crusty bread

CRUNCH SALAD
1 x 5-ounce package prewashed
  watercress
4 pickled onions, or 8 plain cocktail
  onions
1 pear
½ lemon

SEASONINGS
olive oil
extra virgin olive oil
sea salt & black pepper

ETON MESS
1 pound strawberries
1 heaping tablespoon sugar
1 blood orange
2 teaspoons vanilla paste or extract
a splash of Pimm's liqueur
1 cup low-fat yogurt or
  crème fraîche
4 ounces meringue cookies
a couple of sprigs of fresh mint

TO SERVE
English mustard
Good-quality lemonade

TO START Get all your ingredients and equipment ready. Turn the oven on to 425°F and get a grill pan on a high heat. Put the standard blade attachment into the food processor.

SAUSAGE ROLLS Dust a clean surface with all-purpose flour and unroll the puff pastry. Cut the pastry lengthways so that you have two rectangles, each approximately 5x14 inches. Beat the egg in a little bowl, then use a pastry brush to paint the pastry halves. Line the sausages up so you get 6 on each half (just like in the picture). Bash 1 teaspoon of fennel seeds in a pestle & mortar and sprinkle over. Finely grate a layer of Parmesan over the sausages.

Fold the pastry over the sausages, then use a fork to quickly crimp the edges together so you end up with 2 long sausage rolls. Paint these with the rest of the egg wash, then sprinkle over the sesame seeds. Drizzle olive oil over a baking sheet, then roughly cut each long roll into 10 smaller rolls. Lay the rolls on the oiled baking sheet and put into the oven on the top shelf for around 15 minutes, or until golden and puffed up. Wash your hands, then put the loaf of bread for the pâté into the oven to warm through.

ASPARAGUS Trim off and discard the woody ends of the asparagus, quickly rinse the tips, and lay on the hot dry grill pan. Turn occasionally and cook until nicely charred on all sides.

PÂTÉ Put 1 heaping soup spoon of horseradish into the food processor with all of the mackerel and cream cheese, the bunch of parsley, and a good pinch of pepper. Finely grate in the zest of 1 lemon and squeeze in the juice of 1½ lemons. Let the processor run for a few minutes while you wash and halve the radishes and arrange them around the edge of a serving bowl. When everything is quite smooth and well mixed, spoon it into the serving bowl. You can put it into the refrigerator to firm up a bit if you like, but I prefer

it a little softer. Drizzle over some good extra virgin olive oil, then take it to the table with the loaf of warm bread and a lemon half for squeezing over.

ASPARAGUS Turn the asparagus.

CRUNCH SALAD Tip the watercress onto a platter. Thinly slice 4 large pickled onions and sprinkle all around the watercress. Thinly slice the pear into rounds, core and all, then slice the rounds into matchsticks and scatter over. Dress with a good drizzle of extra virgin olive oil and a good pinch of salt & pepper, and take to the table with a lemon half for squeezing over.

ASPARAGUS Drizzle a little extra virgin olive oil over the spears and squeeze over the juice of ½ lemon. Shake the pan, lightly season, then tip everything onto a serving plate. Take to the table with a piece of Cheddar for shaving over.

SAUSAGE ROLLS If they are golden brown and cooked through, take them out of the oven. If not, leave in while you make your dessert.

ETON MESS Slice the strawberries and put them into a bowl with 1 heaping tablespoon of sugar. Grate over the orange zest, then squeeze in the juice from ½ the orange. Add 2 teaspoons of vanilla paste or extract, then really mash and mix everything together with a fork. Add a good splash of Pimm's and mix again. Dollop 2 tablespoons of yogurt or crème fraîche on a platter and spread out, adding the strawberry mixture as you go. Crumble over half the meringue cookies, mix again, then rip some mint leaves over and take to the table with the rest of the meringue cookies – crumble these over just before you serve dessert.

TO SERVE Remove the sausage rolls from the oven, arrange on a platter, and take straight to the table with some English mustard.

CATHERINE WHEEL SAUSAGE

HORSERADISH MASHED POTATOES, APPLE SALAD

SAGE & LEEK GRAVY

STUFFED APPLES

SERVES 4–6

CATHERINE WHEEL SAUSAGE
12 (approx. 1 pound) skinny breakfast
  sausage links, preferably left linked
3 sprigs of fresh sage

GRAVY
2 leeks
a few sprigs of fresh sage
1 organic chicken bouillon cube
1 heaping tablespoon all purpose flour
¾ cup good-quality hard cider

MASHED POTATOES
1¾ pounds Yukon Gold potatoes
a large pat of butter

2 heaping teaspoons
  horseradish sauce

APPLE SALAD
4 multigrain rye crispbreads
3 tablespoons cream cheese
1 lemon
1 small apple
2 cups (2 ounces) prewashed
  watercress

SEASONINGS
olive oil
extra virgin olive oil
sea salt & black pepper

STUFFED APPLES (makes 4 or 6)
4 small apples (or 6 if making for
  6 people)
1 egg
½ cup superfine sugar
1 cup soft dried apricots
¾ cup skinned almonds
heavy cream or plain yogurt, to
  serve
optional: Cointreau, for drizzling

TO SERVE
jar of English mustard
cold hard cider

TO START Get all your ingredients and equipment ready. Turn the broiler to full blast. Put a large saucepan on a low heat. Fill and boil the kettle. Put the standard blade attachment into the food processor.

CATHERINE WHEEL SAUSAGE Scrunch a large sheet of parchment paper under the tap, then lay it out flat. Untwist the links between the sausages and push the meat together to make 2 long sausages. Roll both into one large Catherine wheel. Stab a couple of wooden skewers through, to hold it all together (🍢). Pick the sage leaves and poke them into the gaps. Drizzle with olive oil and rub in. Lift up the parchment paper and transfer the Catherine wheel sausage to a large roasting pan. Tear off any excess paper. Wash your hands. Put the pan under the broiler on the top shelf and cook for 10 minutes, or until the sausage is golden.

STUFFED APPLES Core the apples, then score a line around the middle of each one. Crack the egg into a food processor and add ½ cup superfine sugar, 1 cup soft dried apricots, and ¾ cup skinned almonds. Blitz until combined. Use a spoon to stuff the apples with this mixture, pushing it in from either end. Spread any leftover mixture around the base of a snug-fitting earthenware dish (make sure it's microwave-safe). Set the apples on top, then microwave uncovered for 10 minutes on full power.

GRAVY Put a large frying pan with a lid on a low heat.

MASHED POTATOES Turn the heat under the large saucepan up to high. Quickly cut the potatoes into ½-inch pieces, then put them into the pan and just cover them with boiled water, keeping some water for later. Season with a pinch of salt and put the lid on.

GRAVY Wipe the cutting board. Trim 2 leeks, then halve lengthways and rinse under the tap. Slice into ½-inch thick pieces and add to the empty frying pan with a lug of olive oil and a generous splash of boiled water. Pop the lid on and turn the heat up to medium. Stir occasionally.

CATHERINE WHEEL SAUSAGE By now, the 10 minutes should be up. Take the pan out of the oven, flip over the sausage, and return the pan to the top shelf.

APPLE SALAD Snap 4 rye crispbreads into bite-sized pieces. Use the back of a teaspoon to smear a little cream cheese over each one. Arrange around a platter. Finely grate over the zest of ½ lemon and sprinkle over a little black pepper. Slice off the base of the apple so it sits flat, then slice into rounds as thinly as you can. Stack the slices up and cut across them into matchsticks. Squeeze over the juice of the zested ½ lemon to stop the apple discoloring, and toss.

GRAVY Thinly slice the sage leaves and add to the leeks. Crumble in a chicken bouillon cube and add 1 heaping tablespoon of flour. Stir well and add ¾ cup hard cider. Leave to sizzle away, then add ¾ cup of boiled water. Reduce the heat to low and leave to tick away until you have a good consistency.

APPLE SALAD Put little pinches of watercress among the crispbread pieces. Scatter over the dressed apple. Put the other lemon half on the side for squeezing over, drizzle over a little extra virgin olive oil, and take to the table.

STUFFED APPLES Take the dish of apples out of the microwave. If their stuffing has come out, use a spoon to push it back in. Move the sausage to the bottom shelf of the oven and put the apples on the top shelf to caramelize for the last couple of minutes.

MASHED POTATOES Drain the potatoes in a colander, then return them to the pan and mash with a large pat of butter and a pinch of salt & pepper. Stir in 2 heaping teaspoons of creamed horseradish and take to the table.

STUFFED APPLES Pour the cream into a small pitcher to serve. When golden and delicious, remove the apples from the oven. If you want to be dramatic, like me, drizzle over a splash of Cointreau, then quickly and carefully set alight with a match. Once the flame has burned away, serve with the cream.

TO SERVE Put the sausage on a board and take to the table with the gravy pan. Put a jar of English mustard on the side and dish up. Serve with glasses of cold hard cider.

TAPAS FEAST

SERVES 6

TORTILLA
8 ounces baby white potatoes
1 small red onion
1 teaspoon fennel seeds
2 cloves garlic
½ small bunch of fresh rosemary
8 eggs
a large handful of prepackaged
  arugula, to serve

CHORIZO
8 ounces good-quality cured whole
  chorizo
2 cloves garlic
¼ cup red wine vinegar
1 tablespoon honey

SWEET PEPPERS
4 ounces Manchego cheese
1 ciabatta loaf
⅓ cup skinned almonds
a small bunch of fresh thyme
red wine vinegar
1 x 16-ounce jar whole roasted red
  peppers, packed in oil

MANCHEGO
4 ounces Spanish cured meats, such
  as pata negra
4 ounces Manchego cheese
honey, for drizzling
instant or quality ground coffee
a handful of black olives
optional: a couple of sprigs of fresh
  thyme or oregano

ANCHOVIES
4 ounces marinated white
  anchovies, from the deli counter
a few sprigs of fresh Italian parsley
1 lemon
1 cup cherry or grape tomatoes
smoked paprika, for dusting

SEASONINGS
olive oil
extra virgin olive oil
sea salt & black pepper

TO SERVE
a bottle of sparkling water
1 orange
a chilled bottle of dry sherry

TO START Get all your ingredients and equipment ready. Put a medium ovenproof frying pan (approx. 10 inches) on a high heat and a small frying pan on a low heat. Turn the broiler on to full blast. Put the standard blade attachment into the food processor.

TORTILLA Chop the potatoes into ½-inch chunks. Put them into the medium ovenproof frying pan with a lug of olive oil and toss. Halve, peel, and roughly chop the red onion. Once the potatoes have a good color, add the onions to the pan along with the fennel seeds and mix well. Now get on with other jobs but remember to keep tossing the potatoes occasionally.

CHORIZO Slice the chorizo into 1-inch rounds. Put into the small frying pan with a splash of olive oil and toss occasionally until golden and crisp.

SWEET PEPPERS Trim off the rind from the Manchego, then crumble into the food processor with a handful of torn-up ciabatta, ⅓ cup skinned almonds, the leaves from the bunch of thyme, a good pinch of salt & pepper, and a slug of red wine vinegar. Whiz up until fine, then stuff inside the peppers – no need to pack it in. Once full, put them into a baking dish. Scatter any remaining breadcrumbs over the peppers. Top with the remaining thyme sprigs, drizzle with olive oil, then put on the middle shelf, under the broiler, for 8 minutes. Rip the remaining ciabatta in half and take to the table.

MANCHEGO Lay the slices of cured meat on a board alongside the large wedge of Manchego. Drizzle a little honey over the cheese, then sprinkle over a pinch of ground coffee. Scatter a handful of black olives and a few leaves of thyme or oregano (if using) over the meat. Drizzle with a tiny bit of extra virgin olive oil, sprinkle lightly with pepper and take to the table.

CHORIZO Lightly bash 2 unpeeled cloves of garlic with the heel of your hand or the bottom of a saucepan and add to the pan.

TORTILLA The potatoes should be lovely and golden by now, so turn the heat down to low. Crush 2 unpeeled cloves of garlic into the pan. Pick most of the rosemary leaves into the pan and stir. Season with a good pinch of salt & pepper.

CHORIZO Carefully drain away most of the fat, leaving about 1 tablespoon of it behind. Add the red wine vinegar and honey and leave to reduce down to a really sticky glaze. Keep an eye on it, giving the pan a shake every so often so it doesn't catch.

TORTILLA Taste the potato mixture for seasoning, then crack the eggs directly into the pan and gently stir with a wooden spoon to create a marbled effect. Turn the heat up to medium. Once the eggs start to set around the sides, scatter the rest of the rosemary leaves on top and put under the broiler on the top shelf for 3 to 5 minutes, or until set, golden, and fluffy.

ANCHOVIES Put the anchovies into a nice serving bowl. Finely chop a few sprigs of parsley and sprinkle over. Finely grate over the zest of ½ the lemon, then drizzle over some extra virgin olive oil. Halve the cherry tomatoes and pile them next to the anchovies with a bunch of toothpicks. The idea is to get everyone to make their own skewers. Add a pinch of paprika and take to the table.

TO SERVE Take the tortilla and stuffed sweet peppers to the table. Put a large handful of arugula next to the tortilla. Take the pan of sticky chorizo to the table. Serve with a pitcher of iced sparkling water filled with orange slices, and a chilled bottle of dry sherry.

MOROCCAN LAMB CHOPS

SERVES 4–6

LAMB
2 racks of lamb (8 chops per rack),
   frenched
1 whole nutmeg, for grating
1 teaspoon ground cumin
1 teaspoon sweet paprika, plus extra
   for dusting
1 teaspoon dried thyme
1 lemon

COUSCOUS
1¼ cups couscous
1 fresh red chile
a large bunch fresh Italian parsley
   or mint
1 lemon

GARNISHES
4–6 flatbreads
1 tablespoon dried thyme or oregano
1 cup plain yogurt
1 heaping teaspoon harissa
1 cup hummus
½ lemon

SEASONINGS
olive oil
extra virgin olive oil
sea salt & black pepper

STUFFED SWEET PEPPERS
2 ounces good melting cheese,
   such as Cheddar or fontina
8 small whole roasted red peppers,
   from a jar, packed in oil

DRINK
ice cubes
a few sprigs of fresh mint
½ lemon
1 pomegranate
1 bottle of sparkling water

TO START Get all your ingredients and equipment ready. Fill and boil the kettle. Put a large frying pan on a medium heat. Put a roasting pan in the oven and turn the oven on to 425°F.

LAMB Put the racks of lamb on a sheet of parchment paper over a board and cut each rack in half so you have 4 smaller racks. Quickly score the surface area of each rack in a crisscross fashion, then finely grate over ½ the nutmeg, and sprinkle with the cumin, paprika, and thyme. Massage the flavors into the meat, then put in the hot frying pan with a splash of olive oil. Discard the parchment paper. Turn and color the meat on all sides for around 5 minutes as you get on with the rest of the meal.

COUSCOUS Tip the couscous into a large bowl with a drizzle of olive oil and add just enough boiling water to cover. Season with a pinch of salt, then cover with a plate and set aside for a few minutes.

GARNISHES Lay the flatbreads on a board. Drizzle with olive oil, then sprinkle with salt and dried thyme or oregano. Scrunch up and wet a large piece of parchment paper under the tap and flatten out. Stack up the breads and wrap in the parchment paper, then pop onto the lowest oven shelf to warm through.

LAMB Check the lamb. Once brown, transfer to the hot roasting pan, bones facing up, and put on the top shelf of the oven. Set the timer for 14 minutes for blushing to medium meat, slightly less for rare, and more for well done. Halfway through, turn the racks over. Rinse out the lamb frying pan and wipe clean with paper towels. Put on a low heat.

DRINK Half-fill a large pitcher with ice. Scrunch up a few sprigs of fresh mint and add, squeezing in the juice from ½ lemon. Place a strainer over the pitcher, then halve the pomegranate and really squeeze each half so all the seeds break and the juice pours into the pitcher. Discard what's left behind in the strainer. Top up with sparkling water, stir with a wooden spoon, and take to the table.

STUFFED SWEET PEPPERS Divide the cheese into 8 slices and put 1 slice inside each pepper.

LAMB Turn the racks now, gently shake the pan, and hit it with a good pinch of salt. Return to the oven.

COUSCOUS Seed and finely chop the red chile. Finely chop most of the parsley or mint leaves (reserving a small handful of leaves). Take the plate off the couscous, add the chopped parsley, chile, a few lugs of extra virgin olive oil, and a pinch of salt & pepper. Squeeze in the juice of a lemon. Toss and fluff up with a fork. Taste and adjust until happy, then take to the table.

GARNISHES Put the yogurt into a bowl and swirl in the harissa. Drizzle over a touch of extra virgin olive oil and add a few reserved parsley leaves. Spoon the hummus onto a plate, make a well in the center, and drizzle with extra virgin olive oil. Add a pinch of salt & pepper, a squeeze of the juice from the lemon half, and a pinch of paprika. Take to the table.

STUFFED SWEET PEPPERS Drizzle olive oil into the frying pan you used for the lamb, then add the peppers. Cook for just 1½ to 2 minutes and once the cheese melts, turn the heat off. It's quick and delicious.

LAMB Remove from the oven and transfer to a board to rest for a few minutes.

TO SERVE Tip the peppers onto a plate and scatter over a few parsley or mint leaves. Take the flatbreads out of the oven. Scatter the rest of the parsley over the lamb, cut the lemon into wedges for squeezing over, and serve on the side. Take everything to the table and enjoy!

SPRING LAMB

VEGETABLE PLATTER

MINT SAUCE

RED WINE GRAVY

CHOCOLATE FONDUE

SERVES 4–6

LAMB

1 x 8-bone rack of lamb, frenched
8 ounces boneless lamb leg steak
  (cut ½-inch thick)
3 sprigs fresh rosemary
2 cloves garlic
1 teaspoon Dijon mustard
white wine vinegar
12 ounces cherry tomatoes on the
  vine

GRAVY

4 slices smoked bacon
2 sprigs fresh rosemary
1 heaping tablespoon all-purpose flour
½ glass of red wine

VEGETABLES

1 pound baby white potatoes
8 ounces baby carrots
stalks from a bunch of fresh mint
1 organic chicken bouillon cube
1 pound green beans
½ Savoy cabbage
1 ⅔ cups frozen peas
a pat of butter
½ lemon

MINT SAUCE

leaves from a bunch of fresh mint
¼ cup red wine vinegar
1 tablespoon superfine sugar

SEASONINGS

olive oil
extra virgin olive oil
sea salt & black pepper

FONDUE

1 x 4-ounce bar of good-quality dark
  chocolate (62% cocoa solids, or higher)
1 teaspoon vanilla paste or extract
½ cup milk
4–6 handfuls of mixed fruit, such as
  mango, strawberries, or pineapple

TO START Get all your ingredients and equipment ready. Put a large frying pan and a large saucepan on a high heat. Fill and boil the kettle. Turn the oven on to 425°F.

LAMB Halve the rack of lamb, then season with salt & pepper and add to the frying pan with a lug of olive oil.

VEGETABLES Wash the potatoes and trim the tops of the carrots. Add everything to the large saucepan with a pinch of salt. Rip the leafy tops off the bunch of mint and put aside for the mint sauce. Make sure the band is still around the stalks, then add them to the saucepan. Just cover with boiled water and crumble in the chicken bouillon cube. Put the lid on.

LAMB Drizzle the olive oil straight onto the leg steak. Turn the racks of lamb then put the leg steak in the pan. Sear the ends of the meat and keep coming back to the pan and turning each piece so they brown all over.

Pull the leaves off 3 sprigs of rosemary and put into a pestle & mortar with a good pinch of salt & pepper. Peel the garlic, add to the mortar, and pound really well. Turn the lamb over. Add Dijon mustard to the mortar with a good couple of lugs of olive oil and a slug of white wine vinegar. Mix well.

Make sure all sides of the lamb are seared, then use tongs to transfer all of it to a roasting pan. Pour away most of the fat in the frying pan, then put it back on a very low heat for the gravy. Spoon the dressing from the pestle & mortar over the lamb and put the cherry tomatoes on top. Move everything around until well coated in the dressing. Sprinkle with salt, then put on the top shelf of the oven and set the timer for 14 minutes for blushing to medium meat, slightly less for rare, and more for well done. Turn the racks over halfway through.

GRAVY Thinly slice the bacon and put into the frying pan.

MINT SAUCE Finely chop the reserved mint leaves and add to the unwashed pestle & mortar. Pound, then add the red wine vinegar, sugar, a pinch of salt, and 2 tablespoons of cooking water from the vegetable pot. Muddle together with the pestle, have a taste to check the balance, and add a tiny splash of extra virgin olive oil. Take to the table with a spoon.

GRAVY Turn the heat under the bacon right up and add the leaves from the rosemary. Stir in the flour, red wine, and a few ladles of cooking water.

VEGETABLES Trim the tops from the green beans. Cut the Savoy cabbage half in two and pull off any tatty outer leaves, then discard the stalk. Cut the cabbage into thin wedges. Add the cabbage, beans, and peas to the saucepan, then stir and put the lid back on.

LAMB Turn the lamb over. If your tomatoes are coloring too much, lean the meat on top of them.

GRAVY Stir in a spoonful of cooking water if needed.

FONDUE Smash the bar of chocolate in its wrapping, then unwrap and put it into a small microwave-safe bowl with the vanilla paste or extract, a small pinch of salt, and the milk. Microwave on full power for 1½ minutes, leave to rest for a few seconds, and stir, then microwave for 1 more minute on full power. Meanwhile, chop all your fruit into bite-sized chunks and wedges and pile these on a platter. Take the bowl out of the microwave and stir until all the chocolate has melted, then put the bowl on the platter and take to the table.

LAMB When the 14 minutes are up, take your lamb out of the oven and leave it to rest for a minute.

VEGETABLES Drain the veggies in a colander, then return them to the pan. Drizzle well with extra virgin olive oil, and add a good pinch of salt & pepper and a pat of butter. Squeeze over the juice of ½ lemon and toss well. Tip onto a large serving platter and take to the table.

GRAVY Taste and correct the seasoning, then pour into a gravy boat and take to the table.

TO SERVE Cut the racks into individual chops and slice up the leg steak. Pile on a platter. Move most of the cherry tomatoes to the platter on top of the lamb, mushing the rest into the cooking juices. Stir in a good lug of extra virgin olive oil, then drizzle over the platter and serve.

THANKS

This list gets longer and longer every year but, as always, I'm going to do my very best to not leave anyone out. If I do, please forgive me and let me know so I can get you into the reprint! Thanks, first and foremost, to my beautiful and patient wife, Jools, who is still willing to share a meal with me, even when I'm home later than expected. Love you. Thanks to my kids, Poppy, Daisy, Petal, and — (I haven't met this one yet!) for being such funny, interesting, and generally wonderful little people. Thanks and love as always to Mum and Dad and, of course, to Gennaro Contaldo.

To my dear friend and photographer extraordinaire "Lord" David Loftus: once again, mate, you've outdone yourself. Choosing between all your beautiful photographs this time around has been a real struggle. Much love.

Huge thanks and love to my wonderfully supportive, creative, and energetic food team. You've been excited about this book right alongside me and done an incredible job as usual: to the brilliant style girls Ginny Rolfe, Anna Jones, Sarah Tildesley, Georgie Socratous and little Christina "Scarabooch" McCloskey. Big love to my main men Pete Begg and Daniel Nowland and, of course, to superb ladies Claire Postans, Bobby Sebire, Joanne Lord, Helen Martin, and to Laura Parr for keeping an eye on nutrition for me! I honestly don't know what I'd do without you guys. Big shout out as well to Abigail "Scottish" Fawcett, Becca Hetherston, and Kelly Bowers for their help on recipe testing.

Love and thanks to my hardworking word girls: my editor, Katie Bosher, and the lovely Rebecca "Rubs" Walker and Bethan O'Connor.

Big shout out to the Penguin crew, who are always brave enough to get behind my crazy ideas. Especially to my dear friends John Hamilton, Lindsey Evans, Tom Weldon, and Louise Moore — it has been a pleasure working on another one of these books together. Thanks, as well, to my new mate, Alistair (Al, Aladdin, Aslan, Alsace) Richardson, for his help designing this book. To the rest of the Penguin team who keep the wheels turning and do such a great job under pressure: Nick Lowndes, Juliette Butler, Janis Barbi, Laura Herring, Airelle Depreux, Clare Pollock, Chantal Noel, Kate Brotherhood, Elizabeth Smith, Jen Doyle, Jeremy Ettinghausen, Anna Rafferty, Ashley Wilks, Naomi Fidler, Thomas Chicken, and all the people on their teams – great work, guys. And big thanks, as always, to the very lovely Annie Lee, and to Helen Campbell and Caroline Wilding. This book also has a digital edition with lots of great bonus content. So big thanks, once again, to David Loftus and also to Paul Gwilliams for the beautiful filming they've done for that. Thanks also to Matt Shaw and Gudren Claire from Fresh One for sorting out all the footage and editing it so beautifully. My marketing exec, the very lovely and clever Eloise Bedwell, worked hard to bring all the digital stuff together, so a big shout out to her.

To my CEO, John Jackson, managing director, Tara Donovan, and manager, Louise Holland ("Yoda," "M," or my "Chief of Staff" as she's known in America), and all of their teams – thanks so much for doing what you do so brilliantly. Same goes for my personal team, who do the most incredible job of looking out for me and keeping my life on track: Liz McMullan, Holly Adams, Beth Richardson, Paul Rutherford, Saffron Greening, and Susie Blythe – thanks, guys. The rest of my wonderful office work so hard every day and make coming into work an absolute pleasure. Lots of them got stuck in and tested the recipes in this book for me (a few pictures of them are opposite) so a big round of applause to them for giving me such great feedback. You guys are brilliant! Thanks as well to my PR in America, the fantastic Kimberly Yorio.

And big, big love and thanks to the wonderful television team pictured with me on the opposite page. You guys helped me turn this book into a brilliant series and we had a great time doing it. To my lovely Fresh One team: Zoe Collins and Jo Ralling, Roy Ackerman, Martha Delap, Emily Taylor, Kirsten Rogers, Gudren Claire, Lou Dew, Esub Miah, and Alex Gardiner. The brilliant crew: Luke Cardiff, Dave Miller, Olly Wiggins, Paul Gwilliams (cheers for the extra pics), Mike Sarah, Godfrey Kirby, Daryl Higgins, Andy Young, Pete Bateson, Jeff Brown, and Chris Stevens – you guys really are the best. Shout out again to my incredible food girls who helped make the filming go so smoothly. Big thanks as well to Kate McCullough, Almir Santos, and also to the edit team, Jen Cockburn, Jackie Witts, Barbara Graham, Steve Flatt, and Mike Kerr.

And, of course, a big thanks to the Forster family. The last thing Jools needed while pregnant with our fourth child was me shooting a whole book in our kitchen. So I was very lucky that these guys were willing to let me invade their beautiful home to cook for days on end. Crispin, who's been my favorite carpenter for a few years now, made the table in this book especially for me. Thanks so much, mate, and big hugs to Gemma and your two boys, Jago and Felix. I enjoyed every minute.

INDEX

Page references in **bold** indicate an illustration
v indicates a vegetarian recipe

A

v   affogato: Black Forest affogato   98, **99**

v   alfalfa sprouts: sprout salad   147, 148, **149**

    almonds

v   little frangipane tarts   32, **33**

     Trapani-style rigatoni   41, 42, **43**

v   amazing satay sauce   111, 112, **113**, 114, **115**

    anchovies: rolled anchovies   260–61, 262, **263**

    apples

v   apple salad   258, **259**

v   stuffed apples   258, **259**

    aragula

v   crunchy chicory & watercress salad   32, **33**

v   herby salad   44-5, **46**, **47**, **175**, 176, **177**

v   aragula & Parmesan salad   41, 42, **43**

v   aragula salad   59, 60, **61**, **63**, 122

     warm garden salad   141, 142, **143**

v   watercress salad   136, **137**

v   Asian greens   23, 182, **183**

    Asian-style salmon   186–7, 188, **189**

    asparagus

v   Asian greens   23, 182, **183**

v   dressed greens   150–51, 152, **153**

v   lovely asparagus   250–51, 252, **253**

v   pan-fried asparagus & vine tomatoes   117, 118, **119**

     summer veggies lasagne   48–9, 50, **51**

    avocados

v   chopped salad   221, **222**

v   crunchy veggies & guacamole   78, **79**

v   goddess salad   211, 212, **213**

v   gorgeous guacamole   191, 192, **193**

v   sprout salad   147, 148, **149**

B

v   baby potatoes   **168–9**, 170

v   baby popovers   194–5, 196, **197**

v   baby zucchini salad   191, 192, **193**

    bacon

     liver & bacon   228, **229**

     lovely butter beans & bacon   211, 212, **213**

     meaty mushroom sauce   237, 238, **239**

v   baked potatoes   211, 212, **213**

    bananas

v   banana ice cream   222, **223**

v   cheat's banoffee pie   170, **171**

    beans

v   garlicky beans   237, 238, **239**

     kinda sausage cassoulet   245, 246, **247**

     lovely butter beans & bacon   211, 212, **213**

     rice & beans   107, 108, **109**

v   rogan josh curry   81, 82, **83**

     summer veggies lasagne   48–9, 50, **51**

    beef

     liver & bacon   228, **229**

     meatball sandwich   221, 222, **223**

     rib-eye stir-fry   205, 206, **207**

     roast beef   194–5, 196, **197**

     steak Indian-style   217, 218, **219**

     steak sarnie   201, 202, **203**

     super-fast beef hash   211, 212, **213**

    beets

v   beet salad   202, **203**

v   beets & cottage cheese   160–61, 162, **163**

v   rainbow salad   165, 166, **167**

    berries

v   berries, shortbread & Chantilly cream   91, 92, **93**

v   berry & custard ripple   **227**, 228
v   berry spritzer   **191**, 192
v   1-minute berry ice cream   23, 182, **183**, 184, **185**
     see also blueberries; raspberries; strawberries
     black beans: rice & beans   107, 108, **109**
v   Black Forest affogato   98, **99**
     Bloody Mary mussels   175, 176, **177**, 178–9
     blueberries
v   fruit & mint sugar   112, **113**
v   lychee dessert   188, **189**
v   1-minute berry ice cream   23, 182, **183**, 184, **185**
v   bocconcini di mozzarella: zucchini & bocconcini
     salad   25, 26, **27**
v   bok choi: greens   205, 206, **207**
     branzino & crispy pancetta   181, **182**, 183
     British picnic   250–51, 252, **253**
     broccoli
v   Asian greens   23, 182, **183**
     broccoli orecchiette   25, 26, **27**, 28, **29**
v   dressed greens   150–51, 152, **153**
v   greens   205, 206, **207**
v   my mashy peas   141, 142, **143**
v   warm broccoli salad   245, 246, **247**
     broth: noodle broth   186–7, 188, **189**
v   brownies: quick brownies   152, **153**
v   butter: homemade butter   160–61, 162, **163**
     butter beans
     kinda sausage cassoulet   245, 246, **247**
     lovely butter beans & bacon   211, 212, **213**
v   butternut squash: rogan josh curry   81, 82, **83**

C

     cabbage
v   cabbage salad   117, 118, **119**
v   kimchee slaw   87, 88, **89**
v   minty cabbage   242, **243**
v   pickled cabbage   221, 222, **223**
     carrots
v   carrot salad   81, 82, **83**
v   little carrots   194–5, 196, **197**
v   rainbow salad   165, 166, **167**
v   sweet carrot smash   91, 92, **93**
     cassoulet: kinda sausage cassoulet   245, 246, **247**

     Catherine wheel sausage   237, 238, **239**,
     257, 258, **259**
     cauliflower
     cauliflower macaroni   34–5, 36, **37**
v   rogan josh curry   **81**, 82, **83**
     celery root
     celery root remoulade & prosciutto   231, 232, **233**, 234
v   celery root smash   237, 238, **239**
v   Chantilly cream   91, 92, **93**
v   chapattis   81, 82, **83**
     chard
v   dressed greens   228, **229**
v   greens   96–7, 98, **99**, 100–101
v   chargrilled corn   108, **109**
     cheat's banoffee pie   170, **171**
     cheat's pizza   59, 60, 61, **62**
v   cheat's rice pudding with stewed fruit   126–7,
     128, **129**
     cheese
v   apple salad   258, **259**
v   arugula & Parmesan salad   41, 42, **43**
v   beets & cottage cheese   160–61, 162, **163**
     cauliflower macaroni   34–5, 36, **37**
v   cheesy mushrooms   202, **203**
v   chopped salad   221, **222**
v   crispy halloumi   136, **137**
v   dressed mozzarella   231, 232, **233**
v   limoncello kinda trifle   42, **43**
     Manchego cheese, cured meats & honey   260–61,
     262, **263**
v   mozzarella salad   60, **61**
v   spinach & feta filo pie   71, 72, **73**
v   spinach & paneer salad   217, 218, **219**
     summer veggies lasagne   48–9, 50, **51**
v   wonky summer pasta   44–5, 46, **47**
v   zucchini & bocconcini salad   25, 26, **27**
v   cheesecake: quick lemon & raspberry cheesecake
     66, **67**
     cherries
v   Black Forest affogato   98, **99**
v   squashed cherries & vanilla mascarpone cream
     59, 60, **61**
     Chianti gravy   270, **271**
     chicken
     chicken pie   91, 92, **93**

chicken skewers **111, 112, 113, 114, 115**

crispy chicken **87, 88, 89**

killer jerk chicken **107, 108, 109**

mustard chicken **96–7, 98, 99**

piri piri chicken **121, 122, 123**

stuffed Cypriot chicken **117, 118, 119**

tray-baked chicken **103, 104, 105**

v chickpeas: rogan josh curry **81, 82, 83**

v chilled hibiscus tea **205, 206, 207**

v chili: sweet chili rice **150–51, 152, 153**

v Chinese cabbage: kimchee slaw **87, 88, 89**

chipolatas

Catherine wheel sausage **237, 238, 239**

kinda sausage cassoulet **245, 246, 247**

sausage rolls **250–51, 252, 253**

chocolate

v Black Forest affogato **98, 99**

v chocolate fondue **270, 271**

v coated ice cream **72, 73**

v quick brownies **152, 153**

v silky chocolate ganache **56, 57**

v thick chocolate mousse **136, 137, 138**

v chopped salad **221, 222**

chorizo: glazed chorizo **260–61, 262, 263**

v chunky croutons **78**

ciabatta

v chunky croutons **78**

v garlic bread **55, 56, 57**

v giant croutons **126–7, 128, 129**

meatball sandwich **221, 222, 223**

steak sarnie **201, 202, 203**

Tuscan tomato salad **48–9, 50, 51**

v clementines: silky chocolate ganache **56, 57**

v coated ice cream **72, 73**

cod: tasty crusted cod **141, 142, 143**

coffee

v Black Forest affogato **98, 99**

v coated ice cream **72, 73**

v vanilla ice-cream float **117, 118, 119**

corn

v chargrilled corn **108, 109**

finnan haddie corn chowder **165, 166, 167**

v cottage cheese: beets & cottage cheese **160–61, 162, 163**

v couscous **155, 156, 157**

v herby couscous **264–5, 266, 267**

crackling: crispy crackling **241, 242, 243**

v creamed spinach **103, 104, 105**

v crispy baby potatoes **202, 203**

crispy chicken **87, 88, 89**

crispy crackling **241, 242, 243**

v crispy halloumi **136, 137**

v crispy mushrooms **66, 67**

v crispy potatoes **194–5, 196, 198, 199**

crispy salmon **191, 192, 193**

croutons

v chunky croutons **78**

v giant croutons **126–7, 128, 129**

v crunch salad **250–51, 252, 253**

v crunchy chicory & watercress salad **32, 33**

v crunchy salad **55, 56, 57**

v crunchy veggies & guacamole **78, 79**

v crushed potatoes **242, 243**

v cucumber salad **71, 72, 73, 131, 132, 133**

curry

v curry sauce **217, 218, 219**

green curry **87, 88, 89**

v rogan josh **81, 82, 83**

Thai red shrimp curry **131, 132, 133**

custard

v berry & custard ripple **227, 228**

v peaches 'n' custard **242, 243**

D

dan dan noodles **205, 206, 207**

dauphinoise: quick dauphinoise **96–7, 98, 99**

desserts

v banana ice cream **222, 223**

v berries, shortbread & Chantilly cream **91, 92, 93**

v berry & custard ripple **227, 228**

v Black Forest affogato **98, 99**

v cheat's banoffee pie **170, 171**

v cheat's rice pudding with stewed fruit **126–7, 128, 129**

v chocolate fondue **270, 271**

v coated ice cream **72, 73**

v fresh lemon & lime granita **232, 235**

v   fruit & mint sugar   112, **113**

v   gorgeous rhubarb millefeuille   176, **177**

v   limoncello kinda trifle   42, **43**

v   little frangipane tarts   32, **33**

v   lovely stewed fruit   36, **37**, 38, **39**

v   lychee dessert   188, **189**

v   mango dessert   217, 218, **219**

v   meringues   246, **247**

v   1-minute berry ice cream   182, **183**, 184, **185**

v   papaya platter   132, **133**

v   peaches 'n' custard   242, **243**

v   pear drop tartlets   46, **47**

v   Pimm's Eton mess   252, **253**

v   quick brownies   152, **153**

v   quick lemon & raspberry cheesecake   66, **67**

v   quick mango frozen yogurt in baby cones   50, **52**, **53**

v   silky chocolate ganache   56, **57**

v   squashed cherries & vanilla mascarpone cream   **59**, 60, **61**

v   sticky prune sponge desserts   78, **79**

v   stuffed apples   258, **259**

v   thick chocolate mousse   136, **137**, **138**

v   vanilla ice cream float   117, 118, **119**

v   dips: yogurt dip   217, 218, **219**

v   dressed greens   150–51, 152, **153**, 228, **229**

v   dressed potatoes   122, **123**

  drinks

v   berry spritzer   191, 192

v   chilled hibiscus tea   205, 206, **207**

v   orange & mint tea   155, 156, **157**, 159

v   pomegranate drink   266, **267**

v   raspberry & elderflower slushie   166, **167**

v   St. Clement's drink   117, 118, **119**

v   sparkling lemon ginger drink   182

v   strawberry slushie   103, 104, **105**

  duck salad   126–7, 128, **129**

E

  eggs

v   tortilla   260–61, **262**, **263**

v   wonky summer pasta   44–5, 46, **47**

v   elderflower: raspberry & elderflower slushie   166, **167**

  endive

   Belgian endive salad with insane dressing   34–5, 36, **37**

v   crunchy red endive & watercress salad   32, **33**

v   griddled Belgian endive salad   42, **43**

v   refreshing chopped salad   108, **109**

v   Eton mess: Pimm's Eton mess   252, **253**

F

  fava beans: summer veggies lasagne   48–9, 50, **51**

  fennel

v   crunchy salad   55, 56, **57**

v   fennel & lemon salad   156, **157**, 158

  feta cheese

v   chopped salad   **221**, 222

v   spinach & feta filo pie   **71**, 72, **73**

  fiery noodle salad   111, 112, **113**, 114, **115**

v   figs   136, **137**

  fish

   Asian-style salmon   186–7, 188, **189**

   branzino & crispy pancetta   181, 182, **183**

   crispy salmon   191, 192, **193**

   finnan haddie corn chowder   165, 166, **167**

   fish tray-bake   168–9, 170, 172–3

   grilled sardines   135, 136, **139**

   mackerel pâté   250–51, 252, **253**

   rolled anchovies   260–61, 262, **263**

   seriously good fish tagine   155, 156, **157**

   smoked salmon   160–61, 162, 163

   spaghetti alla puttanesca   55, 56, **57**

   Swedish-style fishcakes   147, 148, **149**

   tasty crusted cod   141, 142, **143**

   see also shellfish

  finnan haddie corn chowder   165, 166, **167**

v   flatbreads   117, 118, **119**, 264–5, 266, **267**

v   fluffy rice   81, 82, **83**

v   focaccia: stuffed focaccia   231, 232, **233–4**

v   fondue: chocolate fondue   270, **271**

  French-style peas   91, 92, **93**

v   fresh lemon & lime granita   232, **235**

v   fresh zingy salsa   147, 148, **149**

v   fruit & mint sugar   112, **113**

G

v garlic bread **55**, 56, **57**
v garlicky beans **237**, 238, **239**
v giant croutons **126–7**, 128, **129**
v ginger: sparkling lemon ginger drink 182
  glazed chorizo **260–61**, 262, **263**
v goddess salad 211, 212, **213**
v gorgeous guacamole **191**, 192, **193**
v gorgeous rhubarb millefeuille 176, **177**
v granita: fresh lemon & lime granita 232, **235**
  gravy
    Chianti gravy 270, **271**
    onion gravy 228, **229**
    sage & leek gravy 257, 258, **259**
    super-quick gravy **194–5**, 196, **197**
v green beans: garlicky beans **237**, 238, **239**
  green curry 87, 88, **89**
v greens **96–7**, 98, **99**, **100–101**, 205, 206, **207**
v   Asian greens 23, 182, **183**
v   dressed greens **150–51**, 152, **153**, 228, **229**
v griddled chicory salad 42, **43**
  grilled sardines **135**, 136, **139**
  guacamole
v   crunchy veggies & guacamole 78, **79**
v   gorgeous guacamole **191**, 192, **193**

H

  haddock
    Swedish-style fishcakes 147, 148, **149**
v halloumi: crispy halloumi 136, **137**
  haricot beans: kinda sausage cassoulet **245**, 246, **247**
  hash: super-fast beef hash 211, 212, **213**
v hazelnuts: coated ice cream 72, **73**
  herbs
v   herby couscous **264–5**, 266, **267**
    herby salad **44–5**, 46, **47**, 175, 176, **177**
    see also individual herbs
v hibiscus: chilled hibiscus tea 205, 206, **207**

  honey: Manchego cheese, cured meats & honey **260–61**, 262, **263**
v horseradish mash 257, 258, **259**

I

  ice cream
v   banana ice cream 222, **223**
v   Black Forest affogato 98, **99**
v   coated ice cream 72, **73**
v   lovely stewed fruit 36, **37**, 38, **39**
v   lychee dessert 188, **189**
v   1-minute berry ice cream 182, **183**, 184, **185**
v   quick mango frozen yogurt in baby cones 50, **52**, **53**
v   vanilla ice cream float 117, 118, **119**

J

v jasmine rice 131, 132, **133**
v jazzed-up rice **191**, 192, **193**
v jerk sauce 107, 108, **109**

K

  kidney: meaty mushroom sauce **237**, 238, **239**
  killer jerk chicken 107, 108, **109**
v kimchee slaw 87, 88, **89**
  kinda sausage cassoulet **245**, 246, **247**

L

  lamb
    Moroccan lamb chops **264–5**, 266, **267**
    spring lamb 269, 270, **271**
  lasagne
    summer veggies lasagne **48–9**, 50, **51**
v   wonky summer pasta **44–5**, 46, **47**
  leeks: sage & leek gravy 257, 258, **259**
v lemonade: sparkling lemon ginger drink 182

lemons
v   fennel & lemon salad   156, **157**, **158**
v   fresh lemon & lime granita   232, **235**
v   quick lemon & raspberry cheesecake   66, **67**
v   St. Clement's drink   117, 118, **119**
lettuce
     French-style peas   91, 92, **93**
v   goddess salad   211, 212, **213**
v   refreshing chopped salad   108, **109**
v   limes: fresh lemon & lime granita   232, **235**
v   limoncello kinda trifle   42, **43**
v   little carrots   194–5, 196, **197**
v   little frangipane tarts   32, **33**
     liver & bacon   228, **229**
v   lovely asparagus   250–51, 252, **253**
     lovely butter beans & bacon   211, 212, **213**
v   lovely stewed fruit   36, 37, **38**, **39**
v   lychee dessert   188, **189**

M

     macaroni: cauliflower macaroni   34–5, 36, **37**
     mackerel pâté   250–51, 252, **253**
     Manchego cheese, cured meats & honey   260–61,
          262, **263**
mangoes
v   mango dessert   217, 218, **219**
v   quick mango frozen yogurt in baby cones
          50, **52**, **53**
mascarpone
v   limoncello kinda trifle   42, **43**
v   squashed cherries & vanilla mascarpone cream
          59, 60, **61**
meat
     Manchego cheese, cured meats & honey   260–61,
          262, **263**
     see also beef; lamb; pork
     meatball sandwich   221, 222, **223**
     meaty mushroom sauce   237, 238, **239**
     melon: prosciutto & melon salad   25, 26, **27**
v   meringues   246, **247**
v   Pimm's Eton mess   252, **253**

v   millefeuille: gorgeous rhubarb millefeuille   176, **177**
mint
v   fruit & mint sugar   112, **113**
v   mint sauce   270, **271**
v   minty cabbage   242, **243**
v   orange & mint tea   155, 156, **157**
v   salsa verde   168–9, **170**
monkfish: seriously good fish tagine   155, 156, **157**
Moroccan lamb chops   264–5, 266, **267**
mozzarella
v   dressed mozzarella   231, 232, **233**
v   mozzarella salad   60, **61**
v   zucchini & bocconcini salad   25, 26, **27**
mushrooms
v   cheesy mushrooms   202, **203**
v   crispy mushrooms   66, **67**
     meaty mushroom sauce   237, 238, **239**
v   oozy mushroom risotto   65, 66, **67**
     mussels: Bloody Mary mussels   175, 176, **177**, **178–9**
     mustard chicken   96–7, 98, **99**
v   my mashy peas   141, 142, **143**

N

v   naan breads   217, 218, **219**
noodles
     dan dan noodles   205, 206, **207**
     fiery noodle salad   111, 112, **113**, 114, **115**
     noodle broth   186–7, 188, **189**
v   rice noodles   87, 88, **89**

O

v   1-minute berry ice cream   182, **183**, **184**, **185**
     onion gravy   228, **229**
v   oozy mushroom risotto   65, 66, **67**
oranges
v   orange & mint tea   155, 156, **157**, **159**
v   St. Clement's drink   117, 118, **119**
     orecchiette: broccoli orecchiette   25, 26, **27**, 28, **29**

P

v pak choi: dressed greens **150–51**, 152, **153**

v pan-fried asparagus & vine tomatoes **117**, 118, **119**

pancetta: sea bass & crispy pancetta **181**, 182, **183**

v paneer: spinach & paneer salad **217**, 218, **219**

v papaya platter 132, **133**

Parmesan cheese

v   arugula & Parmesan salad **41**, 42, **43**

v   wonky summer pasta **44–5**, 46, **47**

parsley

v   herby couscous **264–5**, 266, **267**

v   salsa verde **168–9**, 170

pasta

    broccoli orecchiette **25**, 26, **27**, 28, **29**

    cauliflower macaroni **34–5**, 36, **37**

    pregnant Jools's pasta **31**, 32, **33**

    spaghetti alla puttanesca **55**, 56, **57**

    summer veggies lasagne **48–9**, 50, **51**

    Trapani-style rigatoni **41**, 42, **43**

v   wonky summer pasta **44–5**, 46, **47**

pâté: mackerel pâté **250–51**, 252, **253**

v peaches 'n' custard **242**, **243**

v pear drop tartlets 46, **47**

peas

    French-style peas **91**, 92, **93**

v   greens **205**, 206, **207**

v   my mashy peas **141**, 142, **143**

    summer veggie lasagne **48–9**, 50, **51**

penne: pregnant Jools's pasta **31**, 32, **33**

peppers

v   refreshing chopped salad 108, **109**

v   stuffed sweet peppers **262**, **263**, **264–5**, 266, **267**

v pesto: dressed mozzarella **231**, 232, **233**

v pickled cabbage **221**, 222, **223**

picnic **250–51**, 252, **253**

pies

v   cheat's banoffee pie 170, **171**

    chicken pie **91**, 92, **93**

v   spinach & feta filo pie **71**, 72, **73**

v Pimm's Eton mess 252, **253**

v pineapple: fruit & mint sugar 112, **113**

piri piri chicken **121**, 122, **123**

pizza: cheat's pizza **59**, 60, **61**, 62

Q

v plums

v   cheat's rice pudding with stewed fruit **126–7**, 128, **129**

v   lovely stewed fruit 36, **37**, 38, **39**

v pomegranate drink 266, **267**

v porcini: oozy mushroom risotto **65**, 66, **67**

pork

    crispy crackling **241**, 242, **243**

    meaty mushroom sauce **237**, 238, **239**

    pork chops **241**, 242, **243**

    seared pork fillet **237**, 238, **239**

    see also bacon; pancetta; prosciutto; sausages

potatoes

v   baby potatoes **168–9**, 170

v   baked potatoes **211**, 212, **213**

v   crispy baby potatoes 202, **203**

v   crispy potatoes **194–5**, 196, **198**, **199**

v   crushed potatoes 242, **243**

v   dressed potatoes 122, **123**

v   horseradish mash **257**, 258, **259**

v   my mashy peas **141**, 142, **143**

v   potato salad **160–61**, 162, **163**

v   quick dauphinoise **96–7**, 98, **99**

v   roasted baby potatoes **147**, 148, **149**

v   smashed potatoes 228, **229**

v   squashed potatoes 103, 104, **105**

v   tortilla **260–61**, 262, **263**

pregnant Jools's pasta **31**, 32, **33**

prosciutto

    celeriac remoulade & prosciutto **231**, 232, **233**, **234**

    prosciutto & melon salad **25**, 26, **27**

v prunes: sticky prune sponge desserts 78, **79**

puddings *see* desserts

purple sprouting broccoli

    broccoli orecchiette **25**, 26, **27**, 28, **29**

v   dressed greens **150–51**, 152, **153**

Q

v quick brownies 152, **153**

quick dauphinoise **96–7**, 98, **99**

v quick lemon & raspberry cheesecake 66, **67**

v quick mango frozen yogurt in baby cones 50, 52, 53
v quick Portuguese tarts 122, **123**, **124**

R

v radish sprouts: sprout salad **147**, 148, **149**
    radishes
v   crunchy salad **55**, 56, **57**
v   kimchee slaw **87**, 88, **89**
v rainbow salad **165**, 166, **167**
    raspberries
v   fresh lemon & lime granita 232, **235**
v   limoncello kinda trifle 42, **43**
v   meringues 246, **247**
v   quick lemon & raspberry cheesecake 66, **67**
v   raspberry & elderflower slushie 166, **167**
v red cabbage: pickled cabbage **221**, 222, **223**
    red peppers
v   refreshing chopped salad 108, **109**
v   stuffed peppers 264–5, 266, **267**
v refreshing chopped salad 108, **109**
v rhubarb: gorgeous rhubarb millefeuille 176, **177**
    rib-eye stir-fry **205**, 206, **207**
    rice
v   cheat's rice pudding with stewed fruit 126–7, 128, **129**
v   fluffy rice **81**, 82, **83**
v   jasmine rice **131**, 132, **133**
v   jazzed-up rice **191**, 192, **193**
v   oozy mushroom risotto 65, 66, **67**
    rice & beans 107, 108, **109**
v   rice noodles **87**, 88, **89**
v   sweet chili rice **150–51**, 152, **153**
    rigatoni: Trapani-style rigatoni **41**, 42, **43**
v risotto: oozy mushroom risotto 65, 66, **67**
    roast beef **194–5**, 196, **197**
v roasted baby white potatoes **147**, 148, **149**
v rogan josh curry **81**, 82, **83**
    rolled anchovies **260–61**, 262, **263**
v rye bread & homemade butter **160–61**, 162, **163**

S

  sage & leek gravy 257, 258, **259**
v St. Clement's drink **117**, 118, **119**
  salads
v   apple salad 258, **259**
v   arugula & Parmesan salad **41**, 42, **43**
v   arugula salad **59**, 60, **61**, **63**, 122
v   baby zucchini salad **191**, 192, **193**
v   beet salad 202, **203**
v   cabbage salad **117**, 118, **119**
v   carrot salad **81**, 82, **83**
    chicory salad **34–5**, 36, **37**
v   chopped salad **221**, 222
v   crunch salad **250–51**, 252, **253**
v   crunchy chicory & watercress salad **32**, **33**
v   crunchy salad **55**, 56, **57**
v   cucumber salad **71**, 72, **73**, **131**, 132, **133**
    duck salad **126–7**, 128, **129**
v   fennel & lemon salad 156, **157**, **158**
    fiery noodle salad **111**, 112, **113**, **114**, **115**
v   goddess salad **211**, 212, **213**
v   griddled chicory salad 42, **43**
    herby salad **44–5**, 46, **47**, **175**, 176, **177**
v   kimchee slaw **87**, 88, **89**
v   mozzarella salad 60, **61**
v   potato salad **160–61**, 162, **163**
v   prosciutto & melon salad **25**, 26, **27**
v   rainbow salad **165**, 166, **167**
v   refreshing chopped salad 108, **109**
v   simple spinach salad **168–9**, 170
v   spinach & paneer salad **217**, 218, **219**
v   spinach salad 66, **67**
v   sprout salad **147**, 148, **149**, **186–7**, 188, **189**
v   tomato salad **59**, 60, **61**, **71**, 72, **73**
    Tuscan tomato salad **48–9**, 50, **51**
v   warm broccoli salad **245**, 246, **247**
    warm garden salad **141**, 142, **143**
v   watercress salad 136, **137**, **194–5**, 196, **197**
v   zucchini & bocconcini salad **25**, 26, **27**
  salmon
    Asian-style salmon **186–7**, 188, **189**
    crispy salmon **191**, 192, **193**
    fish tray-bake **168–9**, 170, **172–3**
    smoked salmon **160–61**, 162, **163**

Swedish-style fishcakes 147, 148, **149**

salsas

v   fresh zingy salsa 147, 148, **149**

v   salsa verde **168–9**, 170

sandwiches

    meatball sandwich **221**, 222, **223**

    steak sarnie **201**, 202, **203**

    stuffed focaccia **231**, 232, **233-4**

sardines: grilled sardines 135, 136, **139**

v   satay: amazing satay sauce **111**, 112, **113**, 114, **115**

sauces

v   amazing satay sauce **111**, 112, **113**, 114, **115**

    Chianti gravy 270, **271**

v   curry sauce 217, 218, **219**

    green curry sauce 87, 88, **89**

v   jerk sauce 107, 108, **109**

    meaty mushroom sauce 237, 238, **239**

v   mint sauce 270, **271**

    onion gravy 228, **229**

v   piri piri sauce 121, 122, **123**

    sage & leek gravy 257, 258, **259**

    super-quick gravy **194–5**, 196, **197**

    tartar sauce **141**, 142, **143**

sausages

    Catherine wheel sausage 237, 238, **239**, 257, 258, **259**

    glazed chorizo **260–61**, 262, **263**

    kinda sausage cassoulet 245, 246, **247**

    pregnant Jools's pasta 31, 32, **33**

    sausage rolls **250–51**, 252, **253**

v   Savoy cabbage: minty cabbage 242, **243**

scallops: sticky pan-fried scallops **150–51**, 152, **153**

seared pork fillet 237, 238, **239**

seriously good fish tagine 155, 156, **157**

shellfish

    Bloody Mary mussels 175, 176, **177**, **178–9**

    finnan haddie corn chowder 165, 166, **167**

    fish tray-bake **168–9**, 170, **172–3**

    spiced tiger shrimp 165, 166, **167**

    sticky pan-fried scallops **150–51**, 152, **153**

    Thai red shrimp curry 131, 132, **133**

shrimp

    finnan haddie corn chowder 165, 166, **167**

    fish tray-bake **168–9**, 170, **172–3**

    spiced tiger shrimp 165, 166, **167**

    Thai red shrimp curry 131, 132, **133**

v   silky chocolate ganache 56, **57**

v   simple spinach salad **168–9**, 170

v   slaw: kimchee slaw 87, 88, **89**

slushies

v   raspberry & elderflower slushie 166, **167**

v   strawberry slushie 103, 104, **105**

v   smashed potatoes 228, **229**

smoked salmon **160–61**, 162, **163**

v   soups: tomato soup 77, 78, **79**

spaghetti alla puttanesca 55, 56, **57**

v   sparkling lemon ginger drink 182

spiced tiger shrimp 165, 166, **167**

spinach

v   creamed spinach 103, 104, **105**

v   greens **96–7**, 98, **99**

v   simple spinach salad **168–9**, 170

v   spinach & feta filo pie 71, 72, **73**

v   spinach & paneer salad 217, 218, **219**

v   spinach salad 66, **67**

spring lamb 269, 270, **271**

v   sprout salad 147, 148, **149**, **186–7**, 188, **189**

v   squash: rogan josh curry 81, 82, **83**

v   squashed cherries & vanilla mascarpone cream 59, 60, **61**

v   squashed potatoes 103, 104, **105**

steak

    rib-eye stir-fry 205, 206, **207**

    steak Indian-style 217, 218, **219**

    steak sarnie **201**, 202, **203**

sticky pan-fried scallops **150–51**, 152, **153**

v   sticky prune sponge desserts 78, **79**

stir-fry: rib-eye stir-fry 205, 206, **207**

strawberries

v   meringues 246, **247**

v   Pimm's Eton mess 252, **253**

v   strawberry slushie 103, 104, **105**

v   stuffed apples 258, **259**

stuffed Cypriot chicken 117, 118, **119**

v   stuffed focaccia **231**, 232, **233-4**

v   stuffed sweet peppers 262, **263**, **264–5**, 266, **267**

sub: meatball sandwich **221**, 222, **223**

v   sugar snap peas: greens 205, 206, **207**

summer veggies lasagne **48–9**, 50, **51**
super-fast beef hash 211, 212, **213**
super-quick gravy **194–5**, 196, **197**
Swedish-style fishcakes 147, 148, **149**
v sweet carrot smash **91**, 92, **93**
v sweet chili rice **150–51**, 152, **153**
sweet potatoes
v dressed potatoes 122, **123**
v sweet potato mash 181, 182, **183**
v Swiss chard: greens **96–7**, 98, **99**

tagine: seriously good fish tagine 155, 156, **157**
tapas feast **260–61**, 262, **263**
tartar sauce 141, 142, **143**
v tartlets: pear drop tartlets 46, **47**
tarts
v little frangipane tarts 32, **33**
v quick Portuguese tarts 122, **123**, 124
tasty crusted cod 141, 142, **143**
tea
v chilled hibiscus tea 205, 206, **207**
v orange & mint tea 155, 156, **157**, 159
Thai red shrimp curry 131, 132, **133**
v 3 delish salads 59, 60, **61**
tomatoes
v pan-fried asparagus & vine tomatoes 117, 118,
    119
v tomato salad 59, 60, 61, 71, 72, **73**
v tomato soup 77, 78, **79**
 Tuscan tomato salad **48–9**, 50, **51**
v tortilla **260–61**, 262, **263**
v thick chocolate mousse 136, **137**, 138
Trapani-style rigatoni 41, 42, **43**
tray-baked chicken 103, 104, **105**
v trifle: limoncello kinda trifle 42, **43**
tuna
 spaghetti alla puttanesca 55, 56, **57**
 Swedish-style fishcakes 147, 148, **149**
 Tuscan tomato salad **48–9**, 50, **51**

V
vanilla
v squashed cherries & vanilla mascarpone cream
    59, 60, **61**
v vanilla ice cream float 117, 118, **119**
vegetables
v crunchy veggies & guacamole 78, **79**
 vegetable platter 269, 270, **271**
 see also individual vegetables; salads

W
v warm broccoli salad 245, 246, **247**
warm garden salad 141, 142, **143**
watercress
v apple salad 258, **259**
v crunch salad **250–51**, 252, **253**
v crunchy chicory & watercress salad 32, **33**
v goddess salad 211, 212, **213**
 warm garden salad 141, 142, **143**
v watercress salad 136, **137**, **194–5**, 196, **197**
v wonky summer pasta **48–9**, 50, **51**

Y
yogurt
v quick mango frozen yogurt in baby cones
    50, **52**, **53**
v yogurt dip 217, 218, **219**
v Yorkshire pudding: baby popovers **194–5**, 196, **197**

Z
zucchini
v baby zucchini salad 191, 192, **193**
v rainbow salad 165, 166, **167**
v zucchini & bocconcini salad 25, 26, **27**